Democracy: A Very Short Introduction

VERY SHORT INTRODUCTIONS are for anyone wanting a stimulating and accessible way in to a new subject. They are written by experts, and have been published in 25 languages worldwide.

The series began in 1995, and now represents a wide variety of topics in history, philosophy, religion, science, and the humanities. Over the next few years it will grow to a library of around 200 volumes – a Very Short Introduction to everything from ancient Egypt and Indian philosophy to conceptual art and cosmology.

Very Short Introductions available now:

ANCIENT PHILOSOPHY
    Julia Annas
THE ANGLO-SAXON AGE
    John Blair
ANIMAL RIGHTS
    David DeGrazia
ARCHAEOLOGY   Paul Bahn
ARCHITECTURE
    Andrew Ballantyne
ARISTOTLE   Jonathan Barnes
AUGUSTINE   Henry Chadwick
BARTHES   Jonathan Culler
THE BIBLE   John Riches
BUDDHA   Michael Carrithers
BUDDHISM   Damien Keown
CHOICE THEORY
    Michael Allingham
CLASSICS   Mary Beard and
    John Henderson
CLAUSEWITZ   Michael Howard
CONTINENTAL PHILOSOPHY
    Simon Critchley
COSMOLOGY   Peter Coles
CRYPTOGRAPHY
    Fred Piper and Sean Murphy
DARWIN   Jonathan Howard
DEMOCRACY   Bernard Crick
DESCARTES   Tom Sorell
DRUGS   Leslie Iversen
EIGHTEENTH-CENTURY
    BRITAIN   Paul Langford

EMPIRE   Stephen Howe
THE EUROPEAN UNION
    John Pinder
FASCISM   Kevin Passmore
THE FRENCH REVOLUTION
    William Doyle
FREUD   Anthony Storr
GALILEO   Stillman Drake
GANDHI   Bhikhu Parekh
HEGEL   Peter Singer
HEIDEGGER   Michael Inwood
HINDUISM   Kim Knott
HISTORY   John H. Arnold
HOBBES   Richard Tuck
HUME   A. J. Ayer
INDIAN PHILOSOPHY
    Sue Hamilton
INTELLIGENCE   Ian J. Deary
ISLAM   Malise Ruthven
JUDAISM   Norman Solomon
JUNG   Anthony Stevens
KANT   Roger Scruton
KIERKEGAARD
    Patrick Gardiner
THE KORAN   Michael Cook
LITERARY THEORY
    Jonathan Culler
LOGIC   Graham Priest
MACHIAVELLI
    Quentin Skinner
MARX   Peter Singer

MATHEMATICS   Timothy Gowers
MEDIEVAL BRITAIN
  John Gillingham and
  Ralph A. Griffiths
MUSIC   Nicholas Cook
NIETZSCHE   Michael Tanner
NINETEENTH-CENTURY
  BRITAIN   Christopher Harvie and
  H. C. G. Matthew
PAUL   E. P. Sanders
PHILOSOPHY   Edward Craig
PHILOSOPHY OF SCIENCE
  Samir Okasha
POLITICS   Kenneth Minogue
POSTMODERNISM
  Christopher Butler
POSTSTRUCTURALISM
  Catherine Belsey
PSYCHOLOGY   Gillian Butler and
  Freda McManus
QUANTUM THEORY
  John Polkinghorne
ROMAN BRITAIN   Peter Salway

ROUSSEAU   Robert Wokler
RUSSELL   A. C. Grayling
RUSSIAN LITERATURE
  Catriona Kelly
THE RUSSIAN REVOLUTION
  S. A. Smith
SCHOPENHAUER
  Christopher Janaway
SHAKESPEARE   Germaine Greer
SOCIAL AND CULTURAL
  ANTHROPOLOGY
  John Monaghan and Peter Just
SOCIOLOGY   Steve Bruce
SOCRATES   C. C. W. Taylor
SPINOZA   Roger Scruton
STUART BRITAIN   John Morrill
TERRORISM   Charles Townshend
THEOLOGY   David F. Ford
THE TUDORS   John Guy
TWENTIETH-CENTURY
  BRITAIN   Kenneth O. Morgan
WITTGENSTEIN   A. C. Grayling
WORLD MUSIC   Philip Bohlman

Available soon:

AFRICAN HISTORY
  John Parker and Richard Rathbone
ANCIENT EGYPT   Ian Shaw
ART HISTORY   Dana Arnold
ART THEORY   Cynthia Freeland
ASTRONOMY   Michael Hoskin
ATHEISM   Julian Baggini
THE BRAIN   Michael O'Shea
BRITISH POLITICS
  Anthony Wright
BUDDHIST ETHICS
  Damien Keown
CAPITALISM   James Fulcher
THE CELTS   Barry Cunliffe
CHAOS   Leonard Smith
CHRISTIAN ART   Beth Williamson
CHRISTIANITY   Linda Woodhead

CITIZENSHIP   Richard Bellamy
CLASSICAL ARCHITECTURE
  Robert Tavernor
CLONING   Arlene Judith Klotzko
THE COLD WAR   Robert McMahon
CONTEMPORARY ART
  Julian Stallabrass
THE CRUSADES
  Christopher Tyerman
DADA AND SURREALISM
  David Hopkins
DERRIDA   Simon Glendinning
DESIGN   John Heskett
DINOSAURS   David Norman
DREAMING   J. Allan Hobson
THE EARTH   Martin Redfern
ECONOMICS   Partha Dasgupta

For more information visit our web site

www.oup.co.uk/vsi

Bernard Crick

DEMOCRACY

A Very Short Introduction

OXFORD
UNIVERSITY PRESS

OXFORD

UNIVERSITY PRESS

Great Clarendon Street, Oxford OX2 6DP

Oxford University Press is a department of the University of Oxford.
It furthers the University's objective of excellence in research, scholarship,
and education by publishing worldwide in

Oxford New York

Auckland Bangkok Buenos Aires Cape Town Chennai
Dar es Salaam Delhi Hong Kong Istanbul Karachi Kolkata
Kuala Lumpur Madrid Melbourne Mexico City Mumbai Nairobi
São Paulo Shanghai Singapore Taipei Tokyo Toronto

Oxford is a registered trade mark of Oxford University Press
in the UK and in certain other countries

Published in the United States
by Oxford University Press Inc., New York

© Bernard Crick 2002

British Library Cataloguing in Publication Data

Data available

Library of Congress Cataloging in Publication Data

Data available

ISBN 0-19-280250-X

3 5 7 9 10 8 6 4

Typeset by RefineCatch Ltd, Bungay, Suffolk
Printed in Spain by Book Print S. L., Barcelona

Contents

List of illustrations

The publisher and the author apologize for any errors or omissions in the above list. If contacted they will be pleased to rectify these at the earliest opportunity.

Introduction

Many meanings attach to the word democracy. If there is one true meaning then it is, indeed, as Plato might have said, stored up in heaven; but unhappily has not yet been communicated to us. The word is what some philosophers have called 'an essentially contested concept', one of those terms we can never all agree to define in the same way because the very definition carries a different social, moral, or political agenda. But somehow, nowadays at least, we cannot live without it. In my *In Defence of Politics* 40 years ago I reified 'this most promiscuous word' as if a Greek or Roman nymph – or say Democratia, an Athenian minor deity: 'She is everybody's mistress and yet somehow retains her magic even when a lover sees that her favours are being, in his light, illicitly shared by many another.'

Plato, of course, detested democracy. To him it was the rule of *doxa* over *philosophia*, of opinion over knowledge. The Greek for rule was *kratos*, and *demos* was 'the people', but many other ancient (and modern) writers gave it a pejorative sense, simply the majority as the mob – a powerful, selfish, fickle, and inconsistent beast. His pupil Aristotle took a more tempered view in his book *The Politics*, as we will see. While democracy was for him a necessary condition for good government, it was far from a sufficient condition. If we are talking of justice and of good government then we are talking of a complexity of different concepts, values, and practices, and a complexity that never remains the same. Beatrice Webb was not denying democracy when she said, 'democracy is not the multiplication of ignorant opinions'; she was merely, if somewhat acidly, putting it in its place and demanding ever more educational reform, or simply education.

So we need some scepticism about any claim that some concept of democracy must be the best for all seasons, as well as some irony about how we choose to wear any one suit of ready-made democratic clothing rather than another; and choose we must, even if by default. In democracies, widespread not-choosing can be a dangerous form of choosing. We each have to choose something but it is another question how and why we presume to choose for others. In a broad sense most of us likely to read a book like this live in a system of government that we call 'democratic'. That word can still, or should, as the Greek poet said, 'warm the blood like wine', whereas, say, 'constitutional government' has a smack of the textbook or the law book about it. There are good reasons for saying 'democratic' for all its ambiguities, use and abuse, as will be rehearsed at the end of this book; and there are choices to be made between different systems of democracy as when new governments are set up – say in post-war Germany and Japan, in the new republics of the former Soviet Union, or in devolved governments as in Scotland, Wales, and Northern Ireland. But this does not mean that somehow democracy is an overriding principle in all circumstances (quite apart from the sad fact that it does not exist in most countries of the world). For example, I happen to have been to a lot of meetings in the last few years in which someone gets up and makes a passionate and reasoned demand for 'democratic schools', and I have tartly shot back, 'Nonsense, a school cannot be democratic; but by god many need to be more democratic and some, indeed, are admirably clear examples of autocracy.'

However, in broad terms the number of different usages of 'democracy' that have had any practical effect have not been all that many. By practical effect I mean when there is some congruence between democracy perceived as a set of values and democracy perceived as a set of institutional arrangements. We can see this best if we consider the history both of the values and of the institutions that have been called democratic.

There are two reasons for an initial historical approach. The first is that to understand any human institutions we must know a little of what has gone before, why they were invented or how they have evolved. Even Marx, believing in revolution, said that in order to change the world we must first understand it (even if he was somewhat idealistic or just plain wrong about the possible extent of change, certainly about the timescales involved). The second reason is itself historical. When democracy began to enter into modern politics and society with the American and then the French Revolutions, the leaders of these events looked back to what they took to be Greek and Roman precedents. They were painted and sculpted in classical togas and laurel wreaths, and they gave themselves Greek and Roman pseudonyms (both for provocation and protection) when they set down their reasoned principles and wrote tracts against royal government and oppression. And the particular pseudonyms they adopted told their readers something of where they were coming from – a 'Brutus' was likely to argue for more immediate action than would a constitutionally minded 'Cicero'. For several centuries the revived memory of the Greek city states (the citizen states) and Rome of the republican era had haunted the West, as real fear for some and as speculative hope for others. What had been done before could be done again. And it is always necessary to remember that we are considering a term that has had no meaning at all in most societies for most of human history, and that while most governments in the modern world feel the need to call themselves democratic, many are at or beyond the outer limits of any of the main usages of the term historically.

I like the challenge of this book because to write briefly and to try to simplify without distortion an overwhelmingly important but also

1. Delacroix's *La Liberté guidant le peuple.*

highly complex matter is more difficult than to write at length. So a double word of warning. Three somewhat different stories (or accountings) must run side by side, which I will try to disentangle and relate to each other more carefully at the end. There is democracy as a principle or doctrine of government; there is democracy as a set of institutional arrangements or constitutional devices; and there is democracy as a type of behaviour (say the antithesis of both deference and of unsociability). They do not always go together. Voting for leaders, for instance, is a democratic device; but many medieval monks in a highly autocratic Church elected their own abbots; Viking war bands would elect a new leader if a chief died on campaign, and Horatio tells us that Hamlet's dying breath was to give his vote to Fortinbras to be king of Denmark ('not how we do it in England', but an Elizabethan audience had evidently heard of such oddities as elective monarchy – they did not need programme notes or a chorus to tell them). The second word of warning is that the history of what is meant by democratic has been hard, until very recently, to disentangle from that of 'republic' and 'republican'.

The tradition of Roman republicanism was revived in the 16th and 17th centuries (finding its finest advocacy and analysis in Machiavelli's *Discourses*) and was an animating idea in the American and French Revolutions; and while it was not democratic as most of us would think of democracy, in that it firmly denied that everyone was fit to vote, and gave some good reasons, yet in some senses it was more democratic than many of us today would feel comfortable with because it stressed the *duty* of all who were citizens *to participate actively* in public life and affairs of state (what scholars call 'civic republicanism'). Today we tend to think that we all have the right to do so, if we feel like it, or not, every so often, if we care to, but that the state will provide laws to protect our individual liberties nonetheless (what scholars call 'liberalism'). But it is wrong, as we will see, to attribute this 'falling off' (or widespread confidence that we can safely leave it all to others) only to the late 20th-century consumer society, Thatcherism, or the deification of the market economy. The roots go deeper and are at the heart of the very ambiguity of the terms 'democracy' and 'liberty' and their associated practices. For Benjamin Constant could write in an essay of 1819, 'The Liberty of the Ancients Compared with that of the Moderns':

> The aim of the ancients was the sharing of social power among citizens of the same fatherland: this is what they called liberty. The aim of the moderns is the enjoyment of liberty in private pleasures; and they call liberty the guarantees accorded by institutions to these pleasures.

Recast in modern dress this contradiction will be my conclusion, but with some hopes for a happy enough ending in which we can enjoy both but only if we study how they can coexist as separate entities rather than be fused – by glib words and thus dangerously confused.

Chapter 1
The word and the deed

'In the beginning was the Word'.
Why now, I'm stuck already. I must change that: how?

. . . . .

The Spirit speaks! I see how it must read
And boldly write, 'In the beginning was the Deed.'
(From David Luke's translation of Goethe's *Faust*)

The word democracy need cause the translator no problems.
It comes more or less intact from the Greek into every major
language. The spirit, Mephistopheles, led Faust into real
trouble, of course, by such a dramatic prompt in mistranslating
the great first line of the Gospel of St John. Oh the tragic quest
for novelty rather than sticking to good old truths! But the
unchanged sacred word 'democracy' can cause troubles
enough because it can mean all things to all men as it is
translated into different cultures and its thread is spun for
different purposes.

Let me illustrate this at once in case any reader still hopes for the
one essential true meaning or a definitive definition. Neither
language nor social organization are like that. In 1962 the late
S. E. Finer wrote a book called *The Man on Horseback*. He listed
six of the official titles with which leading military dictators
'have decorated their regimes':

Nasser:	Presidential Democracy
Ayub Khan:	Basic Democracy
Sukarno:	Guided Democracy
Franco:	Organic Democracy
Stroessner:	Selective Democracy
Trujillo:	Neo-Democracy

Easy to mock such wily opportunism, but I would say that, speaking broadly, while three of those were almost purely despotic, resting almost solely on force and fear, the other three were at least overwhelmingly popular with most of their inhabitants.

And Sammy Finer was only writing about military regimes. The Soviet Union, China, and their allies or puppet states all took very seriously their proud description of being 'Peoples' Democracies'. They believed that the working class should be emancipated, should rule over other classes in a time of revolutionary transition until a classless society was achieved, the rule of the people – democracy. However intolerant the actual ruling Communist party elites were of any dissent, however much they monopolized and abused their exercise of power, they had arisen through popular power and discontent and ultimately depended upon popular support, as happily proved the undoing of the Soviet empire – happily, that is, if you cared for liberty and human rights as well as democracy as majority consent; or if you complacently believed that liberty and democracy are inseparable twins. They should be but they are not.

We all, of course, can mock those perversions of 'democracy' by military regimes and others, because most of us are sure that we live in a democracy, using the term to mean almost everything we want – 'all things bright and beautiful': democracy as a civic ideal, as representative institutions, and as a way of life. Asked to define the term, many would say 'majority rule', but will shift a little if challenged, as in a Socratic dialogue or a seminar, to say more realistically 'majority consent'. But few of us would even then want in every case to equate democracy with justice or rights. Take the issue of capital punishment, for instance. For a variety of reasons British politicians override public opinion, which favours capital punishment. If we are a democracy, we are a parliamentary democracy. American politicians are much more 'democratic' from a majoritarian point of view. So some qualifications are needed if a society or a system of government is to be called 'truly' democratic.

Some say that democracy really means liberty, even liberalism or individualism: laws must defend the (democratic) individual against the (democratic) state. Alexis de Tocqueville partly misread the early 19th-century USA to see democracy as almost a synonym for equality, whereas Andrew Carnegie in his bestseller *Triumphant Democracy* used it to celebrate a highly mobile free-enterprise, market society with great differences in wealth but all justifiable as the product of talent driven by the iron laws of evolution. A trade union conference in the 1930s was told by Ernest Bevin that it was not democratic for a minority to continue to question the decisions of the majority after a vote had been taken, and he received the equally sincere and confusing reply from an offending brother that democracy meant that he could say what he liked, how he liked, and when he liked, even against a majority of the Transport and General Workers Union – which was saying a lot in those days. Or democracy may be seen as a political system that puts constitutional restraints even upon a freely elected (hence democratic) government (the most sought-after use, but historically implausible and usually purely rhetorical). Opposed to 'constitutional democracy' are the ideas of 'sovereignty of the people' or 'the general will', which should prevail over formal constitutional limitations interpreted by lawyers. To some democracy meant little more than 'one man one vote' (and now women, of course), to which others would add hopefully 'plus real choices'. And in broad terms, embracing most of these usages, democracy can be seen as a recipe for an acceptable set of institutions, or else as a 'way of life' in which 'the spirit of democracy' becomes at least as important as the peculiarity of the institutions. For some think that the hallmark of such a way of life lies, indeed, in the deed and not the word: people acting and behaving democratically in patterns of friendship, speech, dress, and amusements, treating everyone else *as if* they were an equal.

One used to hear well-meaning liberals say, 'Well at least the Communists claim to be democratic.' But the trouble was that they *were* democratic in the sound historical sense of a majority consenting to be ruled in a broadly popular way and with a type of regime that needed, unlike old autocracies, to mobilize and enthuse the masses. These regimes no longer governed by the ancient and almost universal axiom of power elites in peasant societies, 'let sleeping dogs lie'; and the obverse of the coin, the peasant saying, as in Tennyson's poem, 'men may come and men may go, but I go on for ever'. Modern autocracies and great men and women make new demands on their populations and need their consent, whether natural or induced.

So we must not leap to the conclusion that there is a 'true democracy' which is a natural amalgam of good government as representative government, political justice, equality, liberty, and human rights. For such volatile ingredients can at times be unstable unless in carefully measured and monitored combinations. Is 'good government' or 'social justice' unequivocally democratic, even in the nicest liberal senses? Probably not. Tocqueville wrote in the 1830s of the inevitability of democracy, but warned against 'the dangers of a tyranny of the majority'. Well, perhaps he cared less for democracy than he did for liberty. But even Thomas Jefferson remarked in his old age that 'an elective despotism was not what we fought for'; and Oliver Wendell Holmes, long the great defender of civil liberties on the United States Supreme Court, once said sarcastically 'democracy is what the crowd wants'. John Stuart Mill, whose *Essay on Liberty* and *Considerations on Representative Government* are two of the great books of the modern world, came to believe that *every* adult (yes, women too) should have the vote, but only after compulsory secondary education had been instituted and had time to take effect. Today the politics of the United States and Great Britain become more and more populist: appeals to public opinion rather than to reasoned concepts of coherent policy. Political leaders can cry 'education, education, education', but with their manipulation of the media, sound-bites, and emotive slogans rather than reasoned public debate, Mill might have had difficulty recognizing them as products of an educated democracy. And our media now muddle or mendaciously confuse what the public happens to be interested in with older concepts of 'the public interest'.

'Democracy' may be a promiscuous and often purely rhetorical word and certainly not a single value embracing or overriding all other values in all circumstances, but I am not saying that we live in a world of the Mad Tea-Party in which words 'mean what I say'. There are limits, but these limits are to be found historically in four broad usages or clusters of meaning attached to 'democracy'. These we must briefly examine because they are at the root of our civilization, and of the hope that it will remain civilized and even perhaps (as the 19th century hoped) progress. As we consider them we must be aware of whether we are talking of an ideal or doctrine; or of a type of behaviour towards others; or of certain institutional and legal arrangements. Democracy can refer to all of these together or to each separately.

The first usage is found in the Greeks, in Plato's attack on it and in Aristotle's highly qualified defence: democracy is simply, in the Greek, *demos* (the mob, the many) and *kratos*, meaning rule. Plato attacked this as being the rule of the poor and the ignorant over the educated and the knowledgeable. His fundamental distinction was between knowledge and opinion: democracy is the rule, or rather the anarchy, of mere opinion. Aristotle modified this view rather than rejecting it utterly: good government was a mixture of elements, the few ruling with the consent of the many. The few should have *arete*, excellence, the idealized concept of aristocracy. But many more can qualify for citizenship by virtue of some education and some property (both of which he thought necessary conditions for citizenship). Democracy as a doctrine or ideal unchecked by the aristocratic principle of experience and knowledge was, however, a fallacy – the belief 'that because men are equal in some things, they are equal in all'.

The second usage is found in the Roman republic, in Machiavelli's great *Discourses*, in the 17th-century English and Dutch republicans, and in the early American republic: that good government is mixed government, just as in Aristotle's theory, but that the democratic popular element could actually give greater power to a state. Good laws to protect all are not good enough unless subjects became active citizens making their own laws collectively. The argument was both moral and prudential. The moral argument is the more famous: both Roman paganism and later Protestantism had in common a view of man as an active individual, a maker and shaper of things, not just a law-abiding well-behaved accepter of and a subject to traditional order. But the prudential argument was always there: a state trusted by its people was a stronger state; and a citizen army or militia was more motivated to defend their homeland than hired mercenaries or cautious professionals.

The third usage is found in the rhetoric and events of the French Revolution and in the writings of Jean-Jacques Rousseau. Everyone, regardless of education or property, has a right to make his or her will felt in matters of public concern; and indeed the general will or common good is better understood by any well-meaning, simple, unselfish, and natural ordinary person from their own experience and conscience than by the over-educated living amid the artificiality of high society. Now this view can have a lot to do with the liberation of a class or a nation, whether from oppression or ignorance and superstition, but it is not necessarily connected with or compatible with individual liberties. (In the European 18th and 19th centuries, remember, most people who cared for liberty did not call themselves democrats at all; they called themselves constitutionalists or civic republicans or, in the Anglo-American discourse, Whigs.)

The fourth usage of democracy is found in the American constitution and in many of the new constitutions in Europe in the 19th century and in the new West German and Japanese constitutions following the Second World War, also in the writings of John Stuart Mill and Alexis de Tocqueville: that all can participate if they care (and care they should), but they must then mutually respect the equal rights of fellow citizens within a regulatory legal order that defines, protects, and limits those rights. This is what most people today in the United States, Europe, the Commonwealth, and Japan etc. ordinarily mean by democracy – let us call it 'modern democracy', ideally a fusion (but quite often a confusion) of the idea of power of the people and the idea of legally guaranteed individual rights. The two should, indeed, be combined, but they are distinct ideas, and can prove mutually contradictory in practice. There can be and have been intolerant democracies and reasonably tolerant autocracies. In the modern era of industry, the mass franchise, and mass communications we can find it difficult to combine freedom and popular power.

The invention of democracy and *political* rule, and then the tradition of governing by means of political debate among citizens, has its roots in the practices and thought of the Greek *polis* and the ancient Roman republic. It is not myopically Eurocentric, or rather Graeco-Romano-centric, to see the history and actual alternative usages of 'democracy' thus. It is historical fact. Great empires, large-scale state formations first arose outside whatever land-mass area or mentality is meant by Europe, and universal monotheistic religions arose from the Middle East and Asia; but modern science and democratic ideas and practices first arose in Europe. Science, religion, and democracy all, of course, take on different modalities as they travel, and both influence and are influenced by different historical cultures.

Chapter 2

The place from where we started

We shall not cease from exploration
And the end of all our exploring
Will be to arrive where we started
And know the place for the first time

(T. S. Eliot, *Little Gidding*)

Back to the word. *The Oxford Classical Dictionary* tells us that the word first emerged around the turn of the 5th to 4th centuries BC after revolts in Athens had removed a dynasty of tyrants from power. *Demokratia* was what the word meant: the rule (*kratos*) of the people (*demos*). 'Tyranny' originally simply meant rule by one man, not necessarily in our sense an oppressor, usually a usurper of kings; an individual tyrant could be good, bad, or not so bad. Nonetheless the tyrants were removed by a large number of the inhabitants of a *polis* or city state who were already beginning to think of themselves as *polites*, citizens of that state, that is with legal rights including the right to speak out and be heard and consulted on matters of common interest, the *politeia* or polity. Sophocles caught the tensions of this time of transition in the *Antigone* when Antigone's cousin Haemon argues for her pardon and her life with Creon the *tyrannos* or ruler. What had she done? Every schoolchild once knew that. She had defied his order and buried the body of her rebel brother Polynices in defiance of the law that the corpse of a traitor should be exposed to the vultures and the wolves, not buried in decency with customary rites.

Creon	Then she is not breaking the law?
Creon	Then she is not breaking the law?
Haemon	Your fellow citizens would deny it to a man.
Creon	And the *polis* proposed to teach me how to rule?
Haemon	Ah. Who is it that's talking like a boy now?
Creon	Can any voice but mine give orders in this *polis*?
Haemon	It is no *polis* if it takes orders from one voice.
Creon	But custom gives possession to the ruler.
Haemon	You'd rule a desert beautifully alone.

We still use the language of the *polis*, indeed almost the whole vocabulary of politics, ancient and modern, is Greek or Roman: autocracy, tyranny, despotism, politics and polity, republic, senate, city and citizen, representative, etc., etc., almost the lot except that one distinctively modern and terrible invention, terribly modern both as word and attempted deed, 'totalitarian'. That was a concept unknown and unimaginable in a pre-industrial age and one that would have been impossible but for the invention and spread of democracy as majority power. For both autocrats and despots depended in the main on a passive population; they had no need to mobilize *en masse*, nor was it easy or practical to take the peasantry *en masse* from working the land, nor were peasants much use in war when they were. Napoleon was to say: 'the politics of the future will be the art of mobilising the masses.' Only industrialization and modern nationalism created such imperatives and possibilities.

Democracy a fighting word

If to us 'democracy' is almost always 'a good thing', even if at times somewhat vaguely all things to all men, to the Greeks from the very beginning it was a partisan, fighting word, separating both philosophies of government and social classes. There were counter-coups by aristocratic factions against democratic ways of governing the state, and these factions and their publicists and their sympathizers throughout the centuries saw *demos* not as 'the people' in an honorific sense (as centuries later an aristocrat, Charles James Fox, was to move a toast in the early days of the French Revolution: 'To our sovereign masters, the People'); but rather as *the mob*, the ignorant and vengeful masses, those too poor to have any education that could fit them for public debate and public service; those all too easily swayed by demagogues trading promises for power. Plato in his dialogues venomously denounces democracy as being the rule of opinion over knowledge; only those with philosophical knowledge of the real nature of things were fit to rule – a view hardly popular, if we read him literally (and it is debatable whether we should), except to tyrants or kings. Broadly speaking, he favoured the idealized aristocratic virtues of excellence and personal perfection.

The fundamental democratic ideal was freedom (*eleutheria*). This was seen as both the political liberty, indeed almost the obligation, to participate in decision-making but also the private liberty to live more or less as one pleased. The most important liberty was freedom to speak out for the common good in the public assemblies and freedom to speak and to think as one chose in the privacy of the home or in the *symposia*, the male, social discussion clubs. Equality was prized, but it was legal and political equality, not economic in the least (except in fantasy in some of the dramatic satires and comedies, even equality for women in the *Ecclesiazusai*). And there was also the collective freedom of the city itself from conquest by others. The Greeks as a whole boasted that they were the *eleutheroi*, the free. Not merely were they collectively free (after some difficulties, most obviously, from domination by the Persian emperors), but they held themselves to be morally superior as individuals to those they called *barbaroi*, or barbarians, precisely because the barbarian Persians, however sophisticated, did not enjoy free politics and democracy. It was a cultural distinction, not a racial one: the culture of free men contrasted with the subjects of despotism.

The difficulties and disadvantages of aristocratic rule were many. The claim to have the rule of the wise and the experienced in the business of government had obvious flaws. Aristotle pointed out in his book of lectures *The Politics* and in his studies of constitutions that aristocracy as an ideal too often degenerated into either oligarchy, the rule of the powerful, or plutocracy, the rule of the rich. None the less skill and wisdom were needed in politics and the business of good government. The best answer lay in finding some middle way: the few ruling with the consent of the many, or 'ruling and being ruled in turn'. And, in any case, rule by the few always needed to placate the many, especially for the defence of the state and the conduct of war. In Athenian terms, someone had to pull the oars of the great trireme war galleys, and do so willingly and skilfully; not a job for sullen slaves or time-serving mercenaries but for willing citizens defending *their* city – or expanding its power aggressively.

2. Head of the goddess Minerva, found in Britain. She was the Roman manifestation of Pallas Athena, patron and protector of the *polis* of Athens.

The two faces of democracy

Democratic institutions, however, had their difficulties too, even if the Athenians were to personify democracy as a goddess, Demokratia, and to sacrifice to her alongside Athena, their protector and patron in all things. To involve all those entitled to have a say and to vote (tens of thousands, even if always a minority of the actual inhabitants of a city – women, youths, aliens, and domestic slaves always predominated numerically) meant cumbersome numbers, too many meetings, and frequent rotation of offices. We now call this 'direct democracy', as contrasted to our 'representative democracy' when all most of us do is vote for representatives at, to the Greek mind, dangerously long intervals. Theirs was what has been called a 'face-to-face society'. Indeed they did not believe that democracy was possible except in relatively small city states where everyone knew intimately what was going on. Aristotle even said that a city should be no larger than that the 'voice of the *stentor*, the herald or town-crier could be heard from one side of the city to the other, nor larger than that every citizen could know the character of every other citizen'. (We now know the others in our huge societies through watching television.) Aristotle probably thought that even the small empire of smaller cities that Athens accumulated around the Aegean Sea was their undoing.

The democratic ideal, however, was clear and one great statement of it that survived and echoed down the ages was the Periclean Oration, the speech of Pericles to his fellow Athenians extolling their democracy as recounted by Thucydides in his *History of the Peloponnesian Wars*. Once upon a time every schoolchild in the whole of Europe and the United States, in the new republics of South and Central America also, would have known at least such an extract as this. Study of the classics was rarely politically neutral and often far from reactionary.

> No one, so long as he has it in him to be of service to the state, is kept in political obscurity because of poverty. And, just as our political life

is free and open, so is our day to day life in our relations with each other. We do not get into a state with our next-door neighbour if he enjoys himself in his own way, nor do we give him the kind of black looks which, though they do no real harm, still do hurt people's feelings. We are free and tolerant in our private lives, but in public affairs we keep to the law. This is because it commands our deep respect. . . . Here each individual is interested not only in his own affairs but in the affairs of the state as well: even those who are mostly occupied with their own business are extremely well informed on general politics – this is a peculiarity of ours: we do not say that a man who takes no interest in politics minds his own business, we say that he has no business here at all. We Athenians, in our own persons, take our decisions on policy or submit them to proper discussions: for we do not think that there is an incompatibility between words and deeds; the worst thing is to rush into action before the consequences have been properly debated . . .

Yes, indeed, 'so long as *he* has it in *him*'. Firm and effective belief in the equality of women and in the iniquity of slavery took another two thousand years and more to become general, and is still not universal; but emancipation demanded equal rights in an existing democracy (with all its ambiguities), it did not need to transform or reject democracy; indeed reformers in the 19th and 20th centuries, men and women alike, used democratic arguments. However, note two things. 'We keep to the law', indeed. It is self-evident that there can be no liberty for anyone without order. But the Greek concept of 'law' will seem strange to us, and the practical implications not always clear to them. They did not believe, as the oration might imply, that obedience to law followed from consent given after open public discussion and debate. For the overriding or basic laws were the traditions of the city itself, often attributed to a mythic founder and personified in the legends of its patron gods. These constituted the very identity of the city. To advocate changing these laws could be seen as a terrible offence, almost to advocate a collective suicide of identity, history, and sanctity. But, of course, laws or edicts for the management of the city had to be passed by public debate and could be changed for the sake of the preservation and welfare of the city and its fundamental laws. Edmund Burke, a traditionalist conservative in modern terms, famously said in the 1780s, 'we must reform in order to preserve' – which catches the same distinction, albeit one whose boundaries themselves are always debatable, always contestable, often vague. But do we not anxiously and most often inconclusively debate whether democratic rights should be allowed to those who threaten democracy? The usual answer is to try to distinguish between, once again, words and deeds. But words can be inflammatory and hateful and some violent deeds can be irritating but mainly symbolic, such as demonstrations that are disruptive for a day but pathetically inadequate to threaten general law and order or to bring down a regime as could the people in ancient cities. In language, as on old maps, borderlands are real enough even if there are no precisely positioned border fences.

Yet the admission that must be made about the Periclean Oration, made in all honesty and realism, is that Pericles was – the historians tell us – a kind of democratic dictator. The Greeks had a word for it, a demagogue. But consider what that shrewd statesman and clever demagogue felt he had to say to stir the people to support him. He gave them an ideal picture of themselves. He played on the Athenian popular mind, but that mind was democratic and had to be led or misled in such terms.

Democracy and polity

The other story in Thucydides, however, is a story of democracy unrestrained and of uninhibited class war, on which he implicitly blames the collapse of Athens in those prolonged wars between Athens and Sparta and their allies, colonies, and puppet states: 'when revolutions broke out in city after city' and 'fanatical enthusiasm became the mark of a real man' and bloody revenge became the order of the day both between and within cities, even within families. 'As a result of these revolutions, there was a general deterioration of character throughout the Greek world. The simple way of looking at things, which is so much the mark of a noble nature, was regarded as a ridiculous quality and soon ceased to exist.' His description of the tumults and massacres in Corcyra became almost as famous as the Periclean Oration. 'Our noble ancestors' reading the classics knew that democracy could pull the one way or the other. We too readily think that if it pulls in that path of violent revenge it cannot possibly be 'democracy', or we invoke not a goddess but an adjective – say 'true democracy'.

So I am sorry to tell the authors of many an American college textbook that Aristotle cannot be invoked as 'the father of democratic political thought'. He was aware of the difficulties of an unrestrained democracy. He saw three basic forms of government, each of which had an ideal and a corrupt form. Monarchy was the rule of one, but the monarch had to be perfectly just otherwise the rule degenerated into tyranny (and since a perfectly just man would be, in Greek ontology, a god, it is very doubtful if Aristotle thought this likely). Aristocracy meant literally the rule of the best, but all too often that degenerated into oligarchy (rule of the few) or plutocracy (rule of the rich). Democracy meant the rule of many but all too often degenerated into anarchy. A state was infinitely stronger if rulers were trusted by the people, if they could carry the people with them by free public debate, and at best they had emerged from the people. But a state needed an educated elite who possessed, not Plato's imagined absolute knowledge, but a kind of practical wisdom that was a mixture of education and experience. So democracy was an essential element in good government but by itself was unlikely to yield good government; not impossible but very difficult. The principle of democracy by itself was to Aristotle fallacious: 'the belief that because men are equal in some things they are equal in all'. If the only choice in practice was between aristocratic oligarchy and democracy, then he favoured democracy. But the advantage of an aristocratic element of influence in a city was that possession of modest property allowed leisure and leisure allowed education and the pursuit of knowledge, which was needed for government as much as for science and commerce. Thomas Hobbes was echoing Aristotle, for once, when he said that 'leisure is the mother of philosophy'.

So Aristotle taught that a blending of the aristocratic virtue of knowledge and democratic power and opinion yielded the best possible state. The name for that, if it needed a name – for if it was difficult to decide objectively whether a constitution was aristocratic or democratic, then the state was probably sound, just, and good – was *politeia*, a *polis* or polity: a state that made its decisions in a political not an autocratic manner. But a polity had to respect all interests in the actual state, not just a democratic majority. He said that in his dialogue *The Republic* his teacher Plato made the mistake of trying to reduce everything in the *polis* to a unity; rather it was the case that 'there is a point at which a polis by advancing in unity will cease to be a polis . . . It is as if you were to turn harmony into mere unison, or to reduce a theme to a single beat. The truth is that the polis is an aggregate of many members.'

So while democracy was a supremely important and distinctive element in Greek political life, the life of the free, the *eleutheroi* as contrasted to the *barbaroi*, it was still only an element, a part not the whole, in what later scholars were to call 'mixed government' or the Romans the *via media* – the middle way of republican government, in political life as well as in the ethics of everyday life. As we will see, as recently as the 1900s statesmen and politicians in Britain and the United States could debate whether the democratic element in their constitutions and political systems was too great or too little. To call the whole system 'democratic' was thought either unrealistic extremism or downright misleading. Some might still agree, if for different reasons. 'We find Solon [the legendary creator of the laws of Athens]', said Aristotle, 'giving the people two general functions of electing magistrates to office and of calling them to account at the end of their tenure of office, but not the right of holding office themselves in their individual capacity,' a line which could no longer be held by his day. What now seems very strange is that he also said that election to office was an aristocratic or oligarchical constitutional device, because the people would vote either for the best or for the richest and most powerful, while a democracy would choose its officers of state by lot. Strange? But a democratic franchise in a modern state rarely avoids the creation of a political elite of office holders. Elected members are not elected because they are necessarily of the people but more mundanely because they want to be elected and can attend lots of party meetings and social events in the evenings, and even that in some countries is a somewhat ideal picture compared to money and patronage. Perhaps the best that modern democracies can hope for is not the avoidance of political elites but 'the circulation of elites', as Joseph Schumpeter suggested in his *Capitalism, Socialism and Democracy* (1942). And do we not think it more just to choose juries by lot rather than by election, appointment, application, or examination tests?

However we construe the origins (and ambiguities) of democracy, the governments of the Greek city states could not have survived as long as they did, lacking bureaucracy and with constant rotation of office, succumbing indeed not by internal collapse but to military conquest by Rome, if there had not been an extraordinary dedication to public business by a citizen class. The Greeks believed that citizenship was the highest end of man, and that immortality consisted in being remembered for services to the *polis*. The immortal gods had founded the city states, and mortal men who had preserved these states in times of crisis or who had founded new ones joined the gods on death, transformed into demi-gods. For the Greeks saw no absolute or ontological difference in substance between men and gods that could not be bridged by service to the state. The supreme individual moral virtue was *arete*, a blending of thought and action, neither the one without the other. Homer gives Achilles *arete* as a 'doer of deeds and a speaker of words', super-abundant *arete* indeed since he had had Charon, a centaur, as tutor: someone half-man and half-beast, thus half reason and half compulsive energy. There was no trace of modern notions that all people have inherent rights: rights were only earned by being an active citizen, certainly not a sit-back-and-beg modern consumer democracy. Harsh, however, to those who did not earn their civic keep or were, like women, judged incapable of the duties of citizenship.

The deepest thinking about the nature of political life, its aims, morality, and limits, came out of Greece. But when 'our noble ancestors', as men once said, the English parliament men of the mid-17th century, the Scottish covenanters, the Dutch, the American, the French republicans argued that government need not be autocratic or royal, indeed overthrew such governments, it was to Rome, not to Greece, that they looked back for proof that better forms of government were possible. These forms and principles they called 'republican'. The example of Greek democracy seemed so much better in theory than in practice. Enemies of democracy could find good stories too in the bloodshed and anarchy portrayed by Thucydides and others rather than the tempered reasoning of Aristotle, who found the democratic element in a polity a necessary but not a sufficient condition for justice and good government.

Roman republicanism

The inhabitants of the early city of Rome also saw themselves as a sacred community of men and their gods, who were a pretty interventionist lot. For some reason they helped the inhabitants of Rome become citizens by getting rid of their kings. The Romans had their version of *arete*, which they called *virtus*, a word misleading if translated as 'virtue' in a modern moral sense: it was the specific virtue or element that a citizen should possess to do whatever was needed for the preservation, expansion, and glory of the state. It was closer to 'courage' than 'virtue' and, of course, it comes from the Latin *vir* for man, as in our virile or manly, not virtuous. Almost by definition women were out of the polity, now seen as the republic, the *res-publica*, the things that are common. Of course 'republican' then meant no kings never no more, but it also meant the constitutional beliefs that bound the classes together. There was class warfare at different points in the early republic, but it was never, as for long periods in Greece, generally seen as democracy versus aristocracy, as if possible and absolute alternatives; rather it was about a balance of power between the senatorial class and the people, the *populus*, in the *respublica*. They realized their mutual dependency as a military nation, first threatened and then more and more threatening, conquering and expanding into empire – the rule of one culture over others. Military technology and citizenship were closely related. The highly elaborate tactics and manoeuvres developed by the Romans demanded both intense collective discipline and high individual skill. The aristocrats were officers who fought among their men, not a caste set apart on horseback; and the common soldiers were craftsmen, not badly armed peasants relying on weight of numbers. It is hard to tell which is cause and which is effect: either the *populus*, the people, had to be or could be trusted with arms. The aristocracy had to remain at least to that degree popular. The army and the city mob of Rome itself had to be integrated into the political community. The long and desperate war against Carthage finally cemented this alliance and made the Romans see it, when they and Greek scholars came to write histories, as the key to their power: 'mixed government', neither solely aristocratic nor solely democratic. Polybius described the Roman constitution as 'the Senate proposing, the people resolving, and the magistrates executing the laws'.

The practice, however, was a potent mixture of republican patriotism and harsh and often brutal aristocratic realism, as tersely asserted on the ensigns of the legions and stamped on all military stores: 'SPQR', *Senatus Populusque Romanus* – The Senate and the People of Rome: this union was the basis of their power over their

3. Nineteenth-century image of a centurion on Hadrian's Wall. On the standard is 'SPQR' – the Senate and the People of Rome.

neighbours. That put the frighteners on them that outside intervention could not divide the patricians from the plebeians (the tale of Coriolanus notwithstanding), as had been the story of much of the Greek internal warfare. Cicero sanitized this magisterially as a formula of constitutional law in his famous '*potestas in populo, auctoritas in senatu*', which he said would guarantee a moderate and harmonious system. But he must have known that that was a nice, tactful legal way of putting what was also a grimly realistic maxim of political prudence. The authority of the Senate and the patrician class, who alone composed the Senate, depended on their never forgetting that in the last analysis power lay with the people of the city of Rome. The people collectively could not govern, but they could tear government down. The main constitutional device for enshrining this maxim was the institution of the tribunes who were magistrates elected by the plebeians, the common people. In the early republic they gained authority from actual meetings of the people in a democratic assembly, the *concilium*, but later the assemblies became irregular and eventually ceased to meet; and always the tribunes to be elected by the people had to be of the senatorial class. But tribunes had a power of veto. It was recognized that no commands of the Senate were constitutionally proper, *or likely to be effective in practice*, unless they could carry the people with them. So the aristocrats who sought elections as tribunes had to be or be able to play the demagogue. Their power was ordinarily limited to a single annual term of office, but this was sometimes set aside if no one cared to take the risk of challenging them.

Consuls were annual officers, but during that time they could apply the authority of the Senate which, in turn, limited others in public law but knew no limits itself: they exercised the *imperium* of the former kings, or the collective power of the whole state. While citizens ordinarily were protected by known laws and a reasonably impartial judicial system, *imperium* could override all. *Imperium* or absolute authority did not cease when the Tarquin kings were killed or turned out, but was exercised for the whole community by the Senate and the consuls – albeit with the possibility of veto by the tribunes. Foreign policy was a senatorial matter and not subject, with some famous exceptions, to popular control. Thus the Roman constitution was, in very broad terms, closer to the 18th-century British idea of the sovereignty of parliament rather than either the French idea of sovereignty of the people or the American idea of constitutional restraints upon government. The republican spirit was that of the citizens (*cives*) of the city (*civitas*). The senators might, like English MPs of the unreformed parliament, own huge landed estates; but in the Senate they were in the midst of, at times literally surrounded by, the city and its tumultuous citizens.

Imperium as a shared cultural value carried with it not just authority plus power (limited only by political prudence) within Rome, but an absolute assertion of external authority over others: the states they defeated or who sought their dangerous protection. *Imperium* was also a certain self-confidence or unbending arrogance that the Romans were as famous for as their justice. Some English at the height of empire and American leaders today are of the same character (imperial power does that to people). Economic factors condition the basic divisions of power in a society, but how that power is actually used depends most often on astonishingly independent patterns of values. *Dignitas*, for instance, was the personal value most prized and cultivated by the patrician or senatorial classes; but every commoner also had his *libertas* and was expected to assert and exercise it actively. *Dignitas* was the quality that marked out a great man from a small, but the *libertas* of the small man was freedom to do what the law allowed him to do, free from arbitrary interventions, and not to suffer more than the law allowed him to suffer. Both were adhered to with equal tenacity. Livy describes a Roman gentleman of the old school as being 'as mindful of the *libertas* of others as he was of his own *dignitas*'. The early republic cultivated myths and stories of exemplary simplicity of manners and unselfish patriotism at whatever personal cost. Cincinnatus, general, saviour of his country, disbands his legions and returns to the plough. There were men like that – as Washington after leaving the presidency was hailed as 'the American Cincinnatus'. Later Abraham Lincoln could remark teasingly 'that "Honest Abe" is most useful to Abraham Lincoln'. If returning to the plough was a way of making a political point, the point made was a good one.

The realism of the Romans about the relationships between power and consent can be seen in the office of *dictator*, for dictatorship was a constitutional office in republican Rome. One man (or two men in early practice) had the unfettered *imperium* surrendered to him for the duration of an emergency. If he attempted either to continue in office after an emergency was over or to prolong the emergency artificially in order to retain power ('did Caesar really need to invade Britain or was this yet another of his excuses to hang on to military command?'), he was *ipso facto* an outlaw. Any man had licence to kill him, if they could. Tyrannicide was the most extreme but the greatest political virtue. The Brutus who killed the last king and his descendant who killed the first Caesar were equally honoured in republican writings. If tyrannicide was never likely to be an effective mechanism to restrain the abuse of power, yet the idea shows the desperate intensity with which the Romans pursued two sometimes incompatible values: the survival of the state and personal freedom and honour. The night that John F. Kennedy was assassinated a weeping friend phoned me to say, 'But Bernard, in all this we must never forget that real tyrants should be killed.'

Roman government thus involved both a complex set of institutions and a most elaborate and rationalized set of values, the latter consciously taught, analysed, lauded, and perpetuated in schools, in literature, and in history, both then and in later ages. That Rome, even of the republic, could become an empire without losing, for that reason (for several hundred years at least), her internal freedoms was due to a way of looking at these very values that was revolutionary in the ancient world. The 'Roman way of life' could, they believed, be learned, earned, and adopted by foreigners. It did not depend on the ethnic composition of the original citizens, nor on the blessing and protection of a set of gods who would only work for their own city. Foreigners taken into citizenship could bring their gods with them, so long as both were loyal to Rome. The Romans actually professed to believe that while their city had had an heroic founder, no less than Aeneas, son of King Priam fleeing from Troy, his successors had gathered followers by making the city a refuge for outlaws and exiles. Despite their rigid class structure, this tough-minded respect for ability rather than birth or descent was ingrained right at the heart of the foundation myth that gave the Romans their sense of identity.

The separation of citizenship from race and finally from the divine protection of local gods was to have momentous consequences. Rome could extend citizenship to allies or even to the pacified elite of conquered nations. Roman law gave a priority to the *ius civile*, the laws of the city of Rome itself, but there was also the *ius gentium*, recognitions of the indigenous laws of the *gens*, the tribes, the other peoples and cultures in the empire. Thus the Romans broke from the severe limits of scale of political organization imposed by Greek culture and values. Loyalty was due not just to 'our noble ancestors' but to perpetuating and propagating the idea of republic itself, a civic religion. It was thus a culture more dominated by law and politics than was even the Greek. Finally the republic was torn to pieces by rival power-hungry tribunes or dictators like Pompey, Sulla, and Julius Caesar. The time of the emperors entered in, at first pretending, like Augustus Caesar, to be simply first magistrate and to follow the forms of the republic (by leaving the Senate but coercing or bribing it). But even when all pretence was thrown away and the lawyer Ulpian in his *Institutiones* in the 3rd century AD set down the great formula of autocracy, '*Quod principi placuit legis vigorem habet*' – what pleases the prince has the force of law – he felt he had to add 'because the people of Rome had conferred their *imperium* and power upon him'. That they never did, unless fear, apathy, or the diversions of 'bread and circuses', *panem et circenses*, counted as a donation of power. But that this shred of democratic legitimacy had to be invoked suggests that it also contained a prudential reminder of the fear of popular power. The legions could be recruited from the countryside but the people were still there in the city.

Chapter 3
Republicanism and democracy

It is a nice reckoning
To put all the governing
All the rule of this land
Into one manne's hand.
One wise manne's head
May stand somewhat in stead:
But the wits of many wise
Much better can devise
By their circumspection
And their sage direction
To cause the common weal
Long to endure in heal.

(Skelton, 'Why Come Ye Not to Court?')

From the time of the Greeks until the 18th century we hear no loud or interesting voices speaking of democracy as either a *doctrine* of principles and institutional arrangements to be put into practice ('have we the right institutions?') nor as a *theory* that might help to explain the rise and fall of states ('are we democratic enough or too democratic?'). But if that word is either lost or too frightening to use, even at first by republicans, we do hear something about republics in the Roman manner and strong echoes of Aristotle's argument about the priority of political rule. This must be kept in mind. Democracies can act tyrannically towards individuals and minorities, but not if they act politically: that is, attempting to conciliate all the main interest groups within a state. Political rule is at least a precondition for just and stable democratic regimes.

Political rule

This argument crops up in some, at first sight, unlikely places. A chief justice of the King's Bench of England, caught up in the Wars of the Roses, wrote a manuscript for the Prince of Wales *On the Governance of the Kingdom of England* (even if it had to wait for publication until 1714). In it he said:

> Ther bith ij [two] kindes off kingdoms, of which on is a lordship called in laten *dominium regale*, and that other is called *dominium politicum et regale*. And thai diversen [there difference] in that the first kynge may rule his peple by suche lawes as he makyth hym self ... The secounde kynge may not rule his peple bi other lawes such as thai assenten unto.

His royal master or patron may not have been very interested in the political rather than the absolute manner of rule, but Sir John Fortescue was not making it up. There were two kinds. Parliaments were common in medieval Europe (only in the 16th and 17th centuries did most of them become suppressed). They mainly represented the nobility, the higher clergy, and sometimes city governments (in England 'the Commons' were a somewhat wider social base of the gentry as well as the nobility in the House of Lords) – these were Fortescue's 'peple'. None of this we could reasonably call democratic. But there was potential democratic institutional device at work: that the kings needed the positive assent of these assemblies to make new laws and, above all else, to raise supply and taxes when they could not, especially in times of war, 'live of their own'. Three centuries later this is what gave parliament ascendancy over Charles I, who otherwise did his best to govern without it. And there was then, as in Fortescue's time, usually no one else to gather the taxes than the magnates and gentry summoned to these parliaments. Putting the taxes 'out to farm', that is the crown selling tax-gathering to a contractor, was highly unpopular as well as corrupt. All this was a matter of political power, of course, not of principle; but so it was. A pretty small class were his 'peple', but they were then those who counted politically. The citizen class in Greece and Rome had never been a majority of the inhabitants, not even of the city of Rome itself. But notice that Fortescue says both *politicum* and *regale*. The royal power, like the Roman *imperium* even in the republic, was needed for the defence of the realm and to enforce the laws; and the lawyers held that for these two functions the king's power was absolute. Modern democracies, as we will see, cannot escape the need to have some provision for emergency powers. The two sides of the coin of government are always there, both power and consent.

The political limits on absolutism in England can be shown by an incident in the reign of the 'great king'. A doubtless apprehensive Bishop Gardiner was summoned before Henry VIII at Hampton Court specifically to be asked if the king, like the Roman emperors, could not simply have his 'will and pleasure regarded as law'. From prison in the next reign he wrote a lively if perhaps self-justifying account of the encounter:

Democracy

> The Lord Cromwell was very stout, 'Come on my Lord of Winchester,' quod he (for that conceat he had, what so ever he talked with me, he knewe ever as much as I, Greke or Laten and all), 'Answer the King here,' quod he, 'but speake plainly and directly, and shrink not, man. Is not that,' quod he, 'that pleaseth the King, a lawe? Have ye not ther in the Civill [Roman] Lawe,' quod he, '*quod principi placuit*, and so fourth?' quod he, 'I have somwhat forgotten it now.' I stood still and wondered in my mind to what conclusion this should tend. The King saw me musing, and with earnest gentelnes sayd, 'Aunswere him whether it be so or no.' I would not aunswere my Lord Cromewell, but delivered my speache to the King, and tolde him I had red in dede of kings that had there will alwayes receaved for a lawe, but, I told him, the forme of his reigne,

34

to make the lawes his wil, was more sure and quiet. 'And by thy forme of goverment ye be established,' quod I, 'and it is agreable with the nature of your people. If ye begin a new maner of policye, how it will frame, no man can tell; and how this frameth ye can tell; and I would never advise your Grace to leave a certeine for an uncerteine.' The King turned his back and left the matter after.

A cunning and a good reply. On the one hand, if you are secure enough already, don't risk rocking the boat – the prudential restraints on power; and on the other, the hint that power rests on 'the nature of your people'. Which was? Best not probe too far. Let sleeping dogs lie. Rebellion was always on the cards.

A Machiavellian moment

Thomas Cromwell was among the first in England to have read Machiavelli's *The Prince*. But one wonders if he had also read *The Discourses*, for there the republican Machiavelli emerges. A state is stronger that can carry its people with it and can trust them with arms. A patriotic citizenry fights harder than hired mercenaries. Yes, princely power used ruthlessly is necessary to create a new state, to save one in times of emergency or to restore one whose inhabitants have lost *virtus*, that Greek and Roman patriotic and civic toughness. But to preserve a state through time, power should be spread; a republic is far superior. The greatest single heroes of antiquity, he says, were men who created republics out of unlikely material but then left them to govern themselves. The power of the people is great and needs to be harnessed by being given a share in a balanced constitution: 'Every city should provide ways and means whereby the ambitions of the populace may find an outlet, especially a city which proposes to avail itself of the populace in important undertakings.' At that point Machiavelli brings the political ideas of the Roman republic into the early modern world. His 'important undertakings' were mainly military training for the defence of the city, or for pre-emptive strikes. But what if a traditional state with a peasant economy in our later modern world seeks to industrialize? It will need not merely to train its masses but to ensure their support, in one democratic way or another, especially as they are now dangerously gathered together in cities. He is at that strange cusp of time when progress has to look to a far past to emancipate itself from feudalism and clericalism. Machiavelli half believes, with Plato, that history is cyclical: monarchy degenerates into tyranny, tyranny provokes democratic revolt, but democracy then proves so anarchic that a monarch or prince has to be found or restored, but then his rule degenerates and provokes democratic revolt . . . But he does believe that with political will and skill and some luck (there is always 'Fortuna' in political life, never inevitability) the right balance of forces can be found to preserve a city through time.

He invents or stumbles upon a theory of modern politics that is one of the two main alternative accounts of democratic politics. The most commonly held and seemingly obvious view is that democracies must try to create a popular consensus of values; but it can also be that they are good at and good for managing inevitable, continuing tensions and conflicts of both values and interests. 'Those who condemn the quarrels between the nobles and the plebs, seem to be', he says, 'condemning the very things that were the primary cause of Rome's retaining her freedom.' In every republic there are 'two different dispositions that of the populace and that of the upper class and that all legislation favourable to liberty is brought about by the clash between them'. So, he concludes, 'if tumults led to the creation of tribunes, tumults deserve the highest praise'. Could democratic institutions, I will ask, be a way of rendering inevitable conflicts creative, not just tolerable? (That is what some have optimistically thought a competitive two-party system would ensure.) And Machiavelli can still remind us that 'those republics which in time of danger cannot resort to a dictatorship will generally be ruined'. Even Rousseau was to say that 'the people's first intention is that the state shall not perish'. And Lincoln would air the eternal dilemma: 'Is there in all republics this inherent and fatal weakness? Must a government of necessity be too

4. Machiavelli, author of the republican *Discourses* as well as *The Prince*.

strong for the liberties of its people, or too weak to maintain its own existence?' Thankfully his own conduct both as politician and as war leader answered his own bleak question – 'not necessarily'. However, Machiavelli's republicanism is limited to a world of independent cities. They may combine temporarily to defend themselves against invasion by the kingdom of France or the Habsburg imperial power, but freedom and politics in his analysis were only possible in the Italian cities and German free cities of his day. He even advocated the 'pruning', cutting out, or purging of those *gentiluomini* who by owning large landed estates outside the city lacked civic spirit and identification.

English civil war

So in the Italian city states, as in the Greek city states and in Rome itself, we have been dealing not merely with civic elites who are a small proportion of the total population, but elites who think that they must necessarily be small. The old Aristotelian analysis seemed almost self-evidently true: possession of property creates leisure and leisure creates both education and time for civic activity – the necessary conditions for citizenship. It is in the civil wars of the mid-17th century in the British Isles (not, please, 'the English Civil War') that we first hear clearly a republican, indeed an egalitarian, claim (in the mouths of a faction called 'Levellers') so general that it sounds fully democratic. The Putney debates between elected representatives from the regiments of the victorious New Model Army (called 'agitators') and their generals, Ireton and Cromwell, which had begun on the issue of back pay, soon turned into a profound discussion of the franchise and the whole constitution of the kingdom.

Violent events brought to the surface 'the underworld of largely unrecorded thinking', as Christopher Hill related in his studies of the myth of 'the Norman Yoke'. It was widely believed by the common people that before 1066 the Anglo-Saxon inhabitants of this country had lived as free and equal citizens, giving allegiance to kings, earls, and thanes democratically and conditionally. The Normans had deprived them of their liberties and their freeholds. 'Magna Carta', said Overton, who with Lilburne and Walwyn were the leaders of the Levellers, 'was but a beggarly thing, containing many marks of intolerable bondage and the laws that have been made since by parliaments have in very many particulars made our governments much more oppressive and intolerable'. Magna Carta was, indeed, a treaty or a stand-off between king and barons giving little or nothing to the common people, and the Levellers were irritated that the great ones of the realm and the lawyers made such a song and dance about it.

An extreme faction of Bible fundamentalists called 'the Diggers', because they began communal cultivation of unused land at St George's Hill, Surrey ('The earth is the Lord's and the fruits thereof' plus 'His saints shall inherit the earth'), justified themselves to General Fairfax and his Council of War in December 1649:

> Seeing that the common people of England by joint consent of person and purse have caste out Charles our Norman oppressor, we have by this time recovered ourselves from under his Norman yoke, and the land is to return into the joint hands of those who have conquered – that is the commoners – and the land is to [be] held [back] from the use of them [the commoners] by the hand of any who will uphold the Norman and kingly power still.

This scepticism about the common lawyers' view of Magna Carta, which became one of the great myths of parliamentary government in the 18th and 19th centuries, did not vanish for a long time. Bronterre O'Brien said on a Chartist platform in 1837 'our own ruling class . . . *wrung* their Magna Carta from King John', therefore, he continued, they should do the same.

The Putney debates contain a classic defence of a property-based franchise, because for the first time it has to answer an explicit claim by the common soldiers and their representatives (in the language of the day called 'agitators') that because they had fought voluntarily to preserve common liberties against the king, they had a right to a vote. One Sexby said:

> There are many thousands of us soldiers that have ventured our lives; we have but little property in the kingdom, yet we have a birthright. But it seems to me now that you argue that except a man hath a fixed estate in the kingdom, he has no right in the kingdom. I wonder we were so much deceived. If we had not a right to the kingdom, we were mere mercenary soldiers. There are many in my condition; it may be that they have little property of estate at present, but they have as much birthright as my lords Cromwell and Ireton, as any in this place.

This is moving and forceful, but notice that two quite different arguments are being made. The one is 'fit to fight, fit to vote', essentially that of the Roman republic and of Machiavelli. If you want us to do the fighting for you, you must take us into the polity. That must have had some worrying force behind it. But the other argument was far more radical – 'birthright': being a freeborn Englishman in itself created a right to vote. This appears to challenge the whole ancient and republican edifice of the qualification for citizenship being built upon education and reason (that can only come from education), not military service alone or simply the 'will' of any individual. He appears to be on the edge of inventing or invoking a philosophy of natural rights that would include civil rights, and there was no warrant for this in any contemporary philosophy, nor did the Bible say that we have a right to vote. We are all equal in the sight of God, there is 'neither Greek nor Jew, circumcised or uncircumcised', we are all the children of one heavenly father; but spiritual equality related to salvation does not help us deconstruct in all circumstances the gnomic text 'Render therefore unto Caesar the things which are Caesar's; and unto God the things that are God's'. Ireton and Cromwell plainly saw the appeal to birthright as 'vain and empty words', rhetorical blather, perhaps a claim to be treated justly as a fellow countryman but not to have been given by God or nature (still less by force of arms) an equal voice in determining what was just.

Ireton replied that there was no question but that there should be representatives and that they should be 'elected as equally as possible':

> but the question is whether the election of this representative should be made by all people equally, or among those equals that have an interest and property of England in them. I stand firm to my opinion ... Property is a creation of civil society: in the state of nature there is no property, nor any foundation for any man to enjoy anything but his bare sustenance and survival. Truly, no man can take away from you your birthright, but in civil society there are laws and a constitution as well as birthright, and no man has a birthright to the property of another. If all men shall vote equally, many shall soon pass to take hold of the property of other men.

Which provoked the response from a Colonel Rainborough, 'Sir, I see that it is impossible to have liberty but that all property must be taken away. If it be laid down for a rule, and if you say it, it must be so.' And he cried out, 'The poorest he that is in England has life to live as the greatest he.' This I heard quoted often by Harold Laski and then in the 1950s by Aneurin Bevan as a staple of Left-wing platforms. But unhappily a decade or two later historians began to show from Leveller pamphlets and manifestos that they too believed in a property franchise: servants, apprentices, debtors, and tenants should not have the vote because they would be in the power of another, not capable of *independent* judgement. Rainborough had no desire whatever 'that all property must be taken away'; he was parodying Ireton's *reductio ad absurdum* and was himself arguing for a wider property franchise. 'Independency' grew as a social ideal as well as reflecting the self-image of a large number of commoners who saw themselves collectively as 'the people', but their self-definition excluded large numbers, almost certainly a majority. Democracy is perhaps a step nearer, but paradoxically individualism of this independent (rather than mutually dependent) 'yeoman' kind would long be an obstacle.

Even the philosopher John Locke a generation later could not break the assumed necessary link between property and citizenship, but he added a very bourgeois stipulation against aristocratic and hereditary claims: the possession of property, he said, was justified if it had been taken out of nature and mixed with 'the labour of his body, and the work of his hands', in other words improved. He made clear in his seminal *Second Treatise on Civil Government* that God allows us 'as much [property] as any one can make use of to any advantage of life before it spoils, so much as he may by his labour fix a property in it. Whatever is beyond this', however, 'is more than his share and belongs to others. Nothing was made by God for man to spoil or destroy.' If the English Commonwealth had collapsed yet both ideas and events began to open up new possibilities. The claim to a 'birthright' made in the Putney debates becomes through Locke a widely held belief, especially in the American colonies, that we are all born with a natural right to 'life, liberty and estate', as Locke said. The idea of natural rights is invented. That is what man is (or rather what God has given to man): a bundle of rights. And if these rights are violated by government, people may take back the rights that they have but lent to government. In Locke there is a carefully hedged right of revolution. What is this 'estate'? It seems to be not property right in general (which can be justified in Lockean terms) but a combination of the minimal possession of things that can guarantee our independence, our individual autonomy; and our 'estate' – which had the connotation of status or dignity ('when I came to man's estate', as Feste sings).

The American cause

The American War of Independence was neither a revolution nor fought for democracy, but it was to have revolutionary and democratic consequences. The British system of government in the decades before the war made no pretence whatever to be democratic. There was agitation, very much helped by the example of stirrings in the 13 colonies, for a more equal representation in parliament of what the libertine, demagogue, and reformer John Wilkes called 'the middling men'. Most of their leaders, himself indeed, regarded themselves, with varying degrees of sincerity and cynicism, as 'tribunes of the people' but not of the people. Generally the reformers were called 'the patriots', following the example of those in the American colonies who had protested against royal authority and then were driven to challenge parliament itself. They were patriots because they said that this is our *patria*, our country, our land which we work with our hands. And the English patriots (to whom, of course, Dr Johnson was referring when he rudely said, probably thinking of 'Jack' Wilkes, 'patriotism is the last refuge of a scoundrel') enjoyed the added implication of the term that the king, the court, and the great lords could be derided as too cosmopolitan – German connections and effete French manners. And in this caricature there was an occasional rhetorical whiff of the Norman yoke again. Very few of the reformers favoured universal manhood suffrage, as when Alderman William Beckford addressed the Corporation of London in 1761: 'Gentleman, our constitution is deficient in only one point, and that is that pitiful little boroughs send members to Parliament equal to great cities; and it is contrary to the maxim that power should follow property.' Perhaps it was failure to think through that Whig maxim that made American separation inevitable then, rather than later. Even Wilkes, the hero of the mob, was far closer to Alderman William Beckford than to Tom Paine's 'rights of man'.

The American question revealed a deeper fear doubtless going back to memories of the English civil war and the brief but frightening interlude of extreme republican, *almost* democratic, ideas. A common and obvious suggestion about how to conciliate the restive colonists was to grant them parliamentary representation. Indeed some argued that they should have it as of right, for certainly there should be no taxation without representation. That seemed axiomatic to many English Whigs. William Pitt, Lord Chatham, the great leader in the Seven Years War, had actually argued that the Stamp Act on the American colonies (to pay for their own defence) was unconstitutional, illegal. There could be no taxation without representation. Parliament was not sovereign in all things. This was a powerful argument, but a minority view in parliament. *Hansard* reported an unnamed MP speaking against the repeal of the Stamp Act:

> There can be no doubt that the inhabitants of the colonies are as much represented in parliament as the greatest part of the people in England are, among nine millions of whom there are eight who have no voice in electing members of parliament: every objection therefore to the dependency of the colonies upon parliament, which arises on the ground of representation, goes to the whole present condition of Great Britain.

If we let the American representatives in, we will have to let those eight millions be represented too. They were, of course, held to be well enough 'virtually represented' (Edmund Burke's helpful phrase) by the combined experience and wisdom (called 'prescription') of their betters in parliament. The MP's panic was premature, but the point is that at last we can see conditions arising in which, even if there was no strong movement for democracy (the actual reformers of the day were in much the same mindset as the Levellers, favouring the minimum property franchise that could ensure 'independency'), there is a real fear of democracy arising, not just something read about in old books setting out 'the good old cause'. Those who opposed reform of any kind caricatured the reformers as anarchic democrats. Some reformers when fitted out with that cap began to wear it provocatively, even proudly.

The predominant temper of mind in the American colonies was that of 'independency', an active individualism that linked both the merchant community and the small farmer. 'I am a freeholder and own my own land', as the young man woos his love in the Appalachian folk song. For in nearly all the state assemblies the franchise was already wider than in all but an exceptional few English constituencies, wider not out of democratic sentiment but because of the wide availability of public land. A right to vote based on a 40*s*. a year taxable freehold was common. More people were accustomed to democratic devices of government: voting, petitioning, and public debate; and, increasingly, demonstrations and rioting when ignored. 'The mob cry "Liberty and Property",' wrote home a royal official, 'a sign they are about to fire a warehouse'. The leaders of the protests, which when ignored and when parliament failed to offer any adequate political and constitutional compromise, turned into a claim and struggle for independence, were of a republican rather than a democratic frame of mind. They wanted an active citizenry but one with a minimum property franchise to ensure some education, some responsibility, some stake in the land. These were 'the people', both to the radical Jeffersonians and to the more conservative followers of Washington and John Adams. But they both strongly favoured constitutional government, that is, a written constitution which would be interpreted not by an elected assembly, the Congress, but by a supreme court; and, in the final constitution, a President bound by oath on appointment to enforce the decisions of the courts – even against the executive government and the Congress itself. John Adams famously said that the new constitution was 'a government of laws and not of men'. While the English parliamentarians revered the English constitution, which under the doctrine of parliamentary sovereignty was what they said it was, Adams said that 'sovereignty is very tyranny'. When the Americans called themselves in their state papers a republic, this did not just mean 'no king': it meant government by elected representatives of 'the people'. But again we must pause to construe that resonant word: much as for the Levellers, it meant all adults except those without taxable property and, of course, women, Indians, and slaves. The claim for separation and self-determination was based explicitly on a Lockean notion of the inherent rights of all (worthy) individuals. The excluded categories were silently passed over for another half-century or more.

5. Thomas Jefferson, draughtsman of the Declaration of Independence.

In the new United States Thomas Jefferson, propagating, almost personifying, the cult of 'the common man' designed and built (had built) his own house at Monticello. He used the latest inventions: the stylograph, so that as he wrote one letter delicate levers attached to his pen moved other pens to make copies – no need for a clerk. He invented or modified the 'dumb waiter' and the 'service lift' so that with true republican simplicity he could serve his guests at table himself, while out of sight the slaves below prepared and pushed up the food. (I had to be reminded at table in Tennessee in 1954 that it was part of 'the code' not to discuss 'the Question' in front of 'them', the attentive waiter, of course.)

'Democracy' was invoked, however, in the extraordinary debates in and surrounding the Philadelphia convention that created the new federal constitution of 1787. It was the very height of a kind of writing that had begun in the protest and independence movement that an American scholar, Perry Miller, once called 'citizen literature': reasoned debate about the fundamental aims and devices of government conducted on a level demanding critical intelligence, but in good plain English to reach the ordinary voter. *The Federalist Papers*, written by Publius, of course (Alexander Hamilton and James Madison) was only the finest and most sustained example. The pamphlet literature surrounding the civil wars of the previous century was the sole precedent of such a kind on such scale. The last time that such high-quality public reasoning happened in Britain was over the Irish question and the Lords reform between 1886 and 1914. (Lament the contrast with today in the dumbing down of great issues in the media or the internalizing of them into the arcane language of the academy; the Scots did produce impressive 'citizen literature' on devolution, but few people read it.) In this American 'citizen literature' there were two great issues: the powers of the central government as against the 13 states; and the checks and balances on how far democracy should reign and the franchise reach down.

The Philadelphia debates virtually invented the idea of federalism as an agreed, legally regulated, and binding distribution of power under a written constitution between a central government and provincial governments. Previously the term had had a very loose meaning, mainly relating to such as the Achaean League in ancient Greece, a treaty between independent cities for common institutions and action for limited purposes; like the 18th-century Swiss confederation, the constituent parts were either free to go or each had a veto over the majority. But the American federal constitution defined and assigned certain limited but important powers to the centre, the federal government, while the separate states of the union retained all else (including control of the franchise). How this balance of power has in fact reversed over the years is another story, and was under dispute right from the beginning. To make even that assignment of power to the centre acceptable, both divisions of power and checks and balances were introduced, the executive and the legislature were separated (unlike in parliament). There was both a Senate with equal representation for each state and a Congress proportionate to the enfranchised population of each state. A Bill of Rights was soon added to the constitution specifically to protect the individual liberties of citizens. All this was complicated, although with skill and patience resolvable; but argument over democracy seemed fundamental and crucial. As in the Putney debates a century before, those who had taken up arms felt no disposition to be fobbed off by something like the old parliamentary system even if without a king and now in the hands of their compatriot 'betters'.

Take just the summary report of the debate of 31 May 1787 on how the lower house was to be elected. A sharp division of opinion appears. The conservatives, or the Federalists, as they soon called themselves (stealing the name), argued for indirect election. '*Mr Sherman* (*Conn.*) opposed the election by the people, insisting that it ought to be by the State Legislatures. The people, he said, immediately should have as little to do as may be about the government. They want [lack] information, and are constantly liable to be misled . . . '. '*Mr Gerry* (*Mass.*) The evils we experience

Democracy

flow from the excess of democracy. The people do not want virtue, but are the dupes of pretended patriots . . . He had, he said, been too republican heretofore: he was still however republican, but had been taught by experience the danger of the levelling spirit.' In Massachusetts 'it would seem to be a maxim of democracy to starve the public servants . . . the popular clamour for the reduction of salaries'. But '*Mr Mason (Va.)* argued strongly for the election of the larger branch by the people. It was to be the grand depository of the democratic spirit of the Government. . . . It ought to know and sympathise with every part of the community. He admitted that we had been too democratic, but was afraid that we should incautiously run to the other extreme. We ought to attend to the rights of every class of the people. He had often wondered at the indifference of the superior classes of society to this dictate of humanity and policy'. Note that he says 'policy' as well as 'humanity'; and the same realism makes him admit that there can be too much democracy as well as too little. It is a vital element in good government but not the whole.

However, a Wilson from Pennsylvania, in what seems a fundamental insight into the nature of modern politics, brought the two arguments together, that on federal versus states' power and that on democracy versus a restricted franchise. He 'contended strenuously for drawing the most numerous branch of the legislature immediately from the people. *He was for raising the federal pyramid to a considerable altitude, and for that reason wished to give it as broad a base as possible.* No government could long subsist without the confidence of the people' (my italics).

Looking back on it all many years later in their old age, Thomas Jefferson wrote to his former antagonist John Adams, 'an elective despotism was not what we fought for'. His party had moved from calling themselves Whigs to calling themselves the Democratic-Republican Party, often 'the democracy', claiming to be the true party of the common people and the common man; yet individual *rights* figured in their beliefs and oratory quite as much as majority rights (and power). The meaning of democracy began to expand in popular understanding to include *liberty* and *rights*, but some were still aware, certainly Jefferson himself, that at different times these could be different forces pulling in different directions. In drafting the Declaration of Independence, Jefferson had turned Locke's natural rights of all men from 'life, liberty and estate' (commonly misquoted then and now as 'life, liberty and property') to 'life, liberty and the pursuit of happiness'. 'Jeffersonian democracy' came to mean a political and social cult of 'the common man', the person who could turn his hand to anything. He could work his own land with his own hands, he could read a law book and tracts on the issues of the day, he could present a case competently in a lower court or in a town meeting, and he carried or possessed arms (by constitutional right) to defend the common liberties if needs be. The Jeffersonian would have agreed with Rousseau and Kant that each of us has within himself a common reason and a moral sensibility, general will or conscience – call it what you will – and if we exercise it with humble simplicity, straightforwardly without fashionable or learned artifice, without selfishness but with empathy, we will reach conclusions very similar to those of our neighbours and fellow countrymen. The common man had common sense. A new democratic morality was being born – however much, in practice, honoured in the breach rather than the observance.

So in the War of Independence and in the formation of the new constitution, democracy was not the motivating force, nor did the individual states when left to themselves to confirm or reform existing voting arrangements move towards a democratic, that is a universal white manhood suffrage – the limits of possibility at the time. Not even that. Most state legislatures stayed with variations on the old freeholder franchises. It used to be said that real democracy and extension of the franchise began when the popular hero General Andrew Jackson, from the newly incorporated frontier state of Tennessee, was elected President in 1829; 'a rough diamond and demagogue if ever there was one', feared his opponents. This was the era of so-called 'Jacksonian democracy'.

But historians now point out that Jackson might never have been elected had most men, 'the plain people', not got the vote *already*, not by democratic reforms but by a gradual inflation of land values that made the old 'forty shilling freehold', often unchanged from colonial days, readily obtainable. But it would be cynicism and too simple to say that inflation brought the democratic franchise rather than ideology. For many would like to have raised the qualification but did not dare to try in the new democratic ethos. Both the conduct of politics and the nature of society would never be quite the same again.

'The triumph of democracy', as some contemporaries and some popular historians have called this period, did not guarantee absence of troubles ahead. What if a Democratic majority (by now a party, hijacking that name) in a large number of states wanted to secede from the Union rather than see 'the peculiar institution' of slavery threatened? A true and rare American reactionary, Fisher Ames, more like an English Tory than a judge of the Massachusetts Supreme Court, remarked sardonically: 'Monarchy is like a splendid ship, with all sails set it moves majestically on, but then it hits a rock and sinks for ever. Democracy is like a raft. It never sinks but, damn it, your feet are always in the water.' That is a good metaphor, for a raft, he implies, is simply swept along by the tide or the current; one can with a paddle or a plank steer a little to stay afloat, trim forward direction slightly to left or right, perhaps even slow down or speed up a little, but there is no turning back against the current of democracy.

The French Revolution

Fisher Ames may have had Charles I or Louis XVIII in mind, but in both cases he was wrong, other than for the United States. Monarchy and autocracy did not sink for ever in Europe. After the military defeat of Napoleon came the restoration of monarchy in France. And although American and British ideas of constitutional government dominated the first stage of the French Revolution, the constitutionalists were soon swept aside by the dictatorship of the Jacobin club. The Jacobins called their rule a dictatorship because, following the Roman usage, they saw that office as a claim to use absolute power for the duration of an emergency: the destruction of the old regime – royalist risings in France, the invasion of France by foreign armies seeking to restore the monarchy before the revolution spread, and opposition and conspiracy (both real and imagined) by their opponents in Paris. And dictatorship was, of course, only for the duration of the emergency until the republic was *pure et dure*, purified, strong, secure. This mentality had little time for democracy in the emerging American sense of majority rule blended with liberty, or legally guaranteed individual rights. The revolutionaries went far beyond a justification to the world of the right to independence, such as Jefferson had penned in the language of a universal appeal to reason; they produced a 'Declaration of the Universal Rights of Man' which was incitement to all peoples to cast off kings and aristocracies and a promise to propagate these principles themselves throughout Europe.

On the table of the Jacobin club was the bust of Rousseau. He must not be blamed for their actions but they saw in him a statement of a new and universal principle (albeit one that could not be applied until after the revolution). 'The people' were no longer only those fit to be citizens by virtue of property and education; the people could now be everyone for two impelling reasons. 'Man is born free but everywhere he is in chains,' said Rousseau in *The Social Contract*. Of course this is obviously untrue. We are born helpless and dependent on our mothers. But what he meant was plain: 'man is born for freedom'. If the chains of tyranny and the artificial conventions of hierarchical society are cast off, we will be become free. That is what is natural. The second impelling reason is that by nature we are each and all capable of expressing 'the general will', perhaps best understood as each of us being capable (with a moral effort) of willing generally, not particularly. This *volonté générale* is not the numerical majority, however; it is the common agreement

6. Rousseau inspired by Nature; Robespierre inspired by action.

of all who try honestly, simply, and with deep sincerity to rid themselves of selfishness and the barriers to a natural life imposed by the artificial conventions of society and the arrogance of the learned. In a word, he turns upside down the republican argument that citizenship must be based on property and education. Without these (at least as society has constituted them hitherto) we can become at last ourselves at our best, discover our true nature. (In fact Rousseau advocates a new kind of paternalistic education, but an education in sensibility and personal development, not in knowledge.) Think what you like of the argument, Rousseau for the first time provides a moral justification for democracy. Each of the successive factions in the French Revolution could then proclaim 'the sovereignty of the people'. But the difficulty was, of course (and always is), that someone has to speak for the people. The Jacobins were sure that they spoke for the people and were not much interested in 'artificial' constitutional restraints or what Mill was to call, and the Americans were in fact practising, representative government.

Alexis de Tocqueville began his seminal *L'Ancien Régime et la Révolution en France* (1856) by saying that the French Revolution was a political revolution which resembled a religious one. 'It had every peculiar and characteristic feature of a religious movement; it not only spread to foreign countries, but it was carried there by preaching and by propaganda.' He said it was impossible to conceive of a stranger spectacle 'than that of political revolution which inspires proselytism, which its adherents preach to foreigners with as much ardour and passion as they have shown in enacting it at home . . . As it affected to tend more towards the regeneration of mankind than even towards the reform of France, it roused passions such as the most violent political revolutions had never before excited.' With its proselytism and propaganda (he uses that word, hitherto just an office of the Catholic Church) it terrified its contemporaries, he said, and 'as Islam had done . . . poured its soldiers, its apostles and its martyrs over the face of the earth'.

Like the Roman 'SPQR', 'Liberty, Equality, Fraternity' was on all the banners; liberty was primarily liberty from the crown, the aristocracy, and the Church – individual liberties would come after the revolution was secure; equality was not economic equality but was equality of status as citizens. The form of address became Citoyen Robespierre, Citoyen St Just, Citoyen Danton; but the fraternity was intense and real, among all those working for the same purposes or in the citizen armies that Danton in the June days rallied to defend the republic. St Just glossed it thus in an address to the Assembly:

> It is your task to build a city whose citizens treat one another as friends, guests and brothers. It is your task to re-establish public confidence and to make it understood that revolutionary government means not war or conquests, but the passage from misery to happiness, from corruption to honesty, from bad principles to good principles.

But people came to ask, would the transition never end? A modern conservative historian not surprisingly likened this to Trotsky's doctrine of the need for 'permanent revolution'. Robespierre spoke of the Jacobin ideal aim, 'the peaceful enjoyment of liberty and equality, and the reign of eternal justice', but this could only be embodied in a state 'which grows great by *the constant sharing* of republican sentiments'. In the meantime he said the aim of the revolution must be *la terreur* (violent intimidation) against the enemies of the revolution, but that the terror would be disastrous without patriotism and patriotism powerless without terror. The terror came to mean not merely swift and ruthless action against those who opposed the revolution but against groups or individuals likely to oppose it. Pose though they might as noble Romans in so much of the iconography of the revolution – Robespierre actually said 'There has been no history since the Romans' – the break with Roman republican ideas of legality was for a time complete.

'The aim of constitutional government is to preserve the republic but that of revolutionary government is to create it. The revolution is the war of liberty against her enemies; the constitution is the regime of liberty victorious and peaceable.' Robespierre continued, 'The constitutional government concerns itself chiefly with private liberty and the revolutionary government with public liberty'. And St Just was to cry out, 'Who are those who are not for us but that they are against us!' (a sentence long remembered in revolutionary tradition, so that Hungarians could in the mid-1970s feel a little happy when their dictator or party leader, Kadar, said 'Those who are not against us are for us' – the relative tolerance of a newly prudent autocrat).

Historians now dispute whether the revolution changed French society as much as was once believed. But that is not the point here. The point is that both the moderation of the constitutional Girondists and the anti-constitutional Jacobins had depended on being able to stir and steer popular power. For a while they seemed to be the embodiment of the popular will without any formal democratic institutions. Their power rested on popularity but the people of the cities had shown their power. The French Revolution was always an unfinished business, whether of hope or of fear, to many in Europe in the 19th century; but most governments, whether out of principle or political prudence, saw the need for some reforms of the franchise and some legal protection for freedom of speech and publication. The republican tradition became strong in French society whether out of respect for 'the people' or fear of them. Democracy in America moved towards a liberalism that guaranteed the rights of citizens while making fewer and fewer demands on them. But democracy in France never quite lost the rougher, republican edge of popular power.

Napoleon did not so much betray the revolution, as surviving old Jacobins said, so much as inherit and rationalize its potential. The revolution had unified and centralized a France which in the old regime had been highly provincial and decentralized in its administration. So Napoleon was able to play the Roman role more sensibly than the Jacobins. His great legal reforms, the *Code Napoléon*, restructured traditional, still semi-feudal French law into a more rational and consistent structure based on the principles of Roman law. For if he made himself emperor, it was explicitly in the mode of the first Roman emperor, an Augustus Caesar seeing himself (or insisting on being seen) as the first magistrate protecting the laws of the republic. And the common people of France had discovered patriotism and nationalism in the struggles against the armies of the old monarchies and the old regime, so much so that Napoleon in his wars could count on a *levée en masse* – say mass conscription. Until that time – and in the monarchies too it remained so – conscription had had to be a highly selective business mainly limited to traditionally loyal areas of the countryside, too dangerous to train and arm the urban mob. And in any case conscription could with safety only be pressed on a minority of the male population of military age to supplement the regular army, not to swamp or overwhelm it; the last people you wanted to arm *en masse* were the common people. But in France the revolutionary spirit was still strong and the common people had gained a sense of their power and their worth. Napoleon could trust them with arms because he was seen as the heir to the revolution against the aristocracy, and if he created his own ranks and orders these were (mostly) based on talent not on birth. Public examinations replaced patronage (mostly) for public office. So it is tempting to say that mass conscription was a device of a democratic age – in that oldest sense of democracy, but not for the emerging America – Jefferson's 'the world's best hope' – rapidly distancing itself from initial enthusiasm for French principles.

Chapter 4
Comme disait
M. de Tocqueville

Despotism . . . appears to me to be peculiarly dreaded in democratic times. I should have loved freedom, I believe, at all times, but in the time in which we live I am ready to worship it.

The nations of our time cannot prevent the conditions of men from becoming equal, but it depends upon themselves whether the principle of equality is to lead them to servitude or freedom, to knowledge or barbarism, to prosperity or wretchedness.

(Alexis de Tocqueville, *Democracy in America*)

John Stuart Mill recounted in his *Autobiography* (1873) that it was reading Tocqueville that began the 'shifting of my political ideal from pure democracy, as commonly understood by its partisans, to the modified form of it . . . in my *Considerations on Representative Government*'. For Tocqueville, Mill asserted, gave a more conclusive account of 'the excellencies of democracy' because while accepting its inevitability he pointed to the 'characteristic infirmities' of popular government to show how they might be remedied. Above all he said, Tocqueville sought a protection against democracy 'degenerating into the only despotism of which, in the modern world, there is real danger – the absolute rule of the head of the executive over a congregation of isolated individuals, all equals but all slaves'. This could come from increased centralization. Mill took from Tocqueville the crucial importance of all those institutions intermediary between the state and the individual in maintaining a balance between liberty and democracy. Mill, who had seen beneficial reforms in England so often frustrated by 'unreasoning prejudice . . . of what pretends to be local government but is, too often, selfish mismanagement by a jobbing . . . local oligarchy', now saw some of these local prejudices as some protection against a wholly centralized state; so a case for the reform of local government not for its dismemberment (*plus ça change, plus c'est la même chose*). Whether or not Tocqueville's account of American society in his two great volumes was wholly accurate, his conclusions were of great influence on how people in Europe and the United States perceived the future, and many of his ideas are still relevant. Although not at all a modern Aristotle, his seriousness and conclusions, like those of Mill, deserve special attention.

Alexis de Tocqueville (1805–59), politically liberal and yet temperamentally conservative, was born in Normandy of aristocratic family, but through all his writings and public service sought to persuade his fellow aristocrats to accept the legacy of the revolution, that there was no turning the clock back. They must accept that a growing equality was inevitable but study how liberty could be preserved in an egalitarian age. By 'equality' he meant actual political equality and a growing equality of condition, the democratic 'manners' or ways of behaviour that he found in America; he did not mean economic equality. He gave all too little attention to the dangers of extreme economic inequalities, except to believe that the growth of commerce and market relationships marked the end of the aristocratic ethos and that the bourgeois ethic was essentially moderate and prudent, inimical to oligarchy – but the ghost of Aristotle might have murmured, 'plutocracy?' in his ear. Nonetheless he is the first profound and systematic analyst of the democratic condition, however unlikely a one. A contemporary described him as 'like pious Aeneas, setting forth to found Rome though still weeping for abandoned Dido, "*mens immota manet, lacrymae volvuntur inanes* [Virgil]"', the mind held firm but tears still flowed down.

In 1831 he and a friend, Gustave de Beaumont, accepted a commission from the French government to visit the United States to write a report on reformed prison systems. From this resulted a published report in 1832 but also Tocqueville's great two volumes, *Democracy in America* (1835 and 1840). The broad idea was in his mind before going to America, indeed was largely the reason why he went: 'I confess that in America I saw more than America. I sought there the image of democracy itself, in order to learn what we have to fear or hope from its progress.' Moreover the main themes and hypotheses of his equally influential and long-laboured work, *L'Ancien Régime et la Révolution en France* (1856), were also forming. The two works were part of a single grand design: to establish how the old aristocratic order in France came to collapse; to persuade people of the inevitability of democracy (by which he meant equality of condition); and by studying actual democracy in the United States, where these tendencies had gone furthest, to see, as it were by comparison, the future of Europe and learn how to safeguard its liberties against the unfinished work of the French Revolution. He ended his first volume with a prediction that soon the world would be dominated by two numerically and geographically vast nations standing for different principles, the Americans and the Russians. And he ended the first book with the once so often quoted: 'The nations of our time cannot prevent the conditions of men from becoming equal, but it depends upon themselves whether the principle of equality is to lead them to servitude or freedom, to knowledge or barbarism, to prosperity or wretchedness.'

The dangers of democracy

In his posthumously published *Souvenirs*, Tocqueville was to mock both the view of the politicians that all great events occur through 'the pulling of strings' and that of the grand theorists of his day that they can all be traced to 'great first causes'. He spoke of tendencies rather than 'iron laws' and said that nothing occurs other than in the context of these tendencies, but that however ripe the time,

DEMOCRACY IN AMERICA.

BY

ALEXIS DE TOCQUEVILLE,

AVOCAT À LA COUR ROYALE DE PARIS,
ETC., ETC.

TRANSLATED BY

HENRY REEVE, Esq.

THIRD EDITION.

IN TWO VOLUMES.

VOL. I.

LONDON:
SAUNDERS AND OTLEY, CONDUIT STREET.
1838.

7. **The title page of the first English edition of Tocqueville's masterpiece.**

nothing occurs by itself without the free actions of particular men. Thus he steers between determinism and voluntarism, yet he argued an inevitable historical tendency towards equality. But the form it will take depends on unpredictable human actions; and the success of such actions depends on understanding historical tendencies and sociological circumstances (even if no amount of understanding can replace, rather than guide, political action). He strives to strike a judicious balance between sociological and political explanation, neither giving too much or too little to the influence of abstract ideas on historical events, even if some will always object that examples are picked to suit an argument, rather than that the argument follows from the evidence. Certainly his America is an abstract model, full of brilliant hypotheses and theories relevant to all modern societies, rather than an empirical investigation of a particular country; but equally certainly his research into French provincial archives for his *L'Ancien Régime et la Révolution en France* was not merely original but of lasting value.

From these provincial sources (not everything happens in Paris, London, Berlin, or Washington, even) he was able to formulate theories of lasting importance: that the actual revolution only speeded up a process of centralization long underway; that the time of maximum danger to an old order is when it tries to reform itself; and that the revolution occurred at a time of economic improvement not at a time of peculiarly great hardship. He summed up the last two propositions by saying that men suffer hopelessly under despotism and poverty; they only stir when there are grounds for hope and signs of improvement.

Basic to both his great works is the distinction between liberty and democracy. To understand what had happened in both the French and the American Revolutions, and their consequences, he found it fruitful to use democracy in the classical sense as simply the rule of the majority, which in turn implies an ever-increasing equality of social condition. He treated America as if it was, in broad brush, a kind of middle-class classless society. Democracies may or may not encourage freedom of expression and individual choice in political action. Tocqueville thought that they could lead to greater liberty that ever before, both for general reasons that he states in *Democracy in America* and because of some institutions peculiar to America; but on the other hand many things in democracy uniquely threaten freedom and individualism. He spoke of 'the dangers of the tyranny of the majority', the intolerance of public opinion, the worship of uniformity and mediocrity, the distrust of eccentricity, diversity, and excellence. His aristocratic disdain can flash when he begins a very short chapter headed, 'The Trade of Literature', 'Democracy not only infuses a taste for letters among the trading classes, but introduces a trading spirit into literature'. But he has a point.

His great fears are expressed in a passage in Chapter 6 of Book II that must be read in full to catch the drama of his high theory.

> I seek to trace the novel features under which despotism may appear in the world. The first thing that strikes the observation is an innumerable multitude of men, all equal and alike, incessantly endeavouring to procure the petty and paltry pleasures with which they glut their lives. Each of them, living apart, is as a stranger to the fate of all the rest; his children and his private friends constitute to him the whole of mankind. As for the rest of his fellow citizens, he is close to them, but he does not see them; he touches them, but he does not feel them; he exists only in himself and for himself alone; and if his kindred still remain to him, he may be said at any rate to have lost his country. Above this race of men stands an immense and tutelary power, which takes upon itself alone to secure their gratifications and to watch over their fate. That power is absolute, minute, regular, provident, and mild. It would be like the authority of a parent if, like that authority, its object was to prepare men for manhood; but it seeks, on the contrary, to keep them in perpetual childhood: it is well content that the people should rejoice, provided they think of nothing but rejoicing. For their happiness such a

government willingly labours, but it chooses to be the sole agent and the only arbiter of that happiness; it provides for their security, foresees and supplies their necessities, facilitates their pleasures, manages their principal concerns, directs their industry, regulates the descent of property, and subdivides their inheritances: what remains, but to spare them all the care of thinking and all the trouble of living.

This passage is rhetorical, over the top, wholly un-PC, and more than a little snobby to modern tastes; and the picture of social isolation is *un peu exagéré* (even if many modern sociologists have talked in somewhat similar terms of 'the lonely crowd', 'alienation', 'anomie', or 'bowling alone'). But it is fully serious and forces us to think of basic issues rather than the next election results or what the neighbours think. This passage has been misread as a prophecy of mid-20th-century totalitarianism – ignoring the 'provident and mild'; but it is quite the contrary. He is not saying that individuals will be ideologized and mobilized for action by a leader or a party, rather they will be dumbed down to lose any interest in corporate political action. It is more like Orwell's sardonic picture of the proles in *Nineteen Eighty-Four*, who were debased into impotence and irrelevance by officially produced 'prolefeed' quite as much as terror (a satire on his today quite as much as our tomorrows). Perhaps Tocqueville's passage has something in common with an old-fashioned Conservative's critique of the likely effects of the welfare state, which now unhappily seems so much more generally accepted that the people have lost their grip on it. But it is also a possible critique of the consumer society.

The advantages and defences of democracy

In the first volume he set out his worries more fully and less rhetorically in a chapter headed 'The Omnipotence of the Majority in the United States and Its Effects', but it was preceded by 'The Real Advantages Derived by American Society from Democratic Government'; then followed a chapter 'The Main Cause to Maintain a Democratic Republic in the United States'. The advantages the Americans had were partly historical. The revolution had been fought to preserve the ideas that the colonists had of their original and inherent freedom. There has not been the bitterness or the violent break of social continuity such as had occurred in France. He saw trouble ahead on the slavery issue which he judged incompatible with the general American ideas of democracy and liberty, but he shrewdly saw the slave population as wanting to enjoy those rights rather than to destroy them as coming from a tainted source. There was widespread respect for the law in the United States and for individual rights, and the constitutional law and the legal profession protected those rights – he was somewhat sanguine about the actual capabilities and impartiality of the small town lawyer. But above all he noted the public-spiritedness of most Americans, so noticeable to other travellers in that era of the early republic, and their willingness to turn their hands to almost anything – the cult of the common man, what later came to be called the 'can do' spirit. There was precariously emerging, he said, using Jefferson's own words, a 'natural aristocracy of talent and virtue', despite 'the tyranny of public opinion'. These men could preserve the aristocratic virtues of skill and excellence from being swept away with the old regimes of privilege and social hierarchy.

Above all else he noted the absence of centralized administration, the prevalence of effective local self-government, the number and independence of the Protestant churches and the many voluntary associations and mutual-aid clubs. He built what was a new theory of politics upon, not the sovereignty of the state, not the sovereignty of the people, which the Jacobins had claimed to embody, but something that later writers called pluralism. Democracy was not a direct relationship between 'the people' and the state (Jacobinism) or between individuals and the state (liberalism), but rather a continuous interplay between intermediary groups, the state, and individual rights. Previous thinkers of the modern age had denounced intermediary groups as frustrating order or reform: Hobbes had spoken of 'corporations' as 'worms within the entrails of the body politic' and 'if there had not been an opinion that powers could be divided, England would not have fallen into the late civil war'; Rousseau had hated them as feudal relics subverting the general will of the common people; and Bentham lumped them all together as 'sinister interests' obstructing uniform and rational legislation aimed at the greatest happiness of the greatest number, not at the promotion of corporate interests. But Tocqueville saw benefit in diversity:

> An association for political, commercial or manufacturing purposes, or even for those of science and literature, is a powerful and enlightened member of the community . . . which, by defending its own rights against the encroachments of government, saves the common liberties of the country.

Yet he said that the question of whether a society is pluralistic or monolithic is only partly an objective question of prior history. The moral factor is always present. Different attitudes can be taken to the same events. He simply argues that if one is serious about liberty in a democracy then much diversity of group interests has to be tolerated, however undemocratic that may sometimes seem. He also distinguishes between centralization of government and of administration. To him it was both necessary and desirable that a democratic government should be active and powerful – within constitutional limits, of course. He said that 'our object should not be to render it weak and indolent but solely to prevent it from abusing its aptitude and strength', and this means the retention and encouragement of provincial and local administration.

Always he stresses choice. In the final book of *Democracy in America* he sums up his argument free from the, at times, diverting detail about American life of the first and more famous volume. His thesis emerges simply and clearly that history presents us with alternatives, and we have to choose. Freedom is moral freedom: choosing and acting after considering the facts of a case in such a way that the scope for free choices by others is at least not impaired, and 'others' are groups as well as individuals. We may not always act that way, we commonly do not. We may not wish to challenge majority opinion, or we may perversely think that it is the true and *authentic* mark of individuality to be doing so all the time. But Tocqueville is simply saying that we should choose to act one way or another, choose morally and knowledgeably, and that in so doing if we treat other people as equal people, then so may they treat us.

There are no protective devices that can be copied exactly from one country to another, or if so are likely to yield the same result. Histories and cultures are different. But the American example was sufficient to show that a conscious and rational allegiance to some laws and customs could restrain even the majority itself. No laws work without will behind them; but mere goodwill is useless without institutions. So to Tocqueville, as to Aristotle, action and understanding must go hand in hand. Individuals are only themselves at their best when acting with others. The state is strong when its roots are deep and local, and allegiance is conditional. American federalism was not the antithesis of power. English Tory polemicists in the early 19th century constantly predicted the collapse of the United States because, amid the checks and balances and divisions of power, there was no clear source of sovereignty. But federalism, Tocqueville implies, is a very strong source of power. Freedom is not the antithesis of authority; it is the only source of authority which can be accepted without force or deception. He seems to conclude that democracy can be lived with to advantage if the right balance can be struck between democratic majoritarianism and liberty.

Perhaps he made his point so well, or shows as theorists often do the logic of how others reach the same conclusion independently, that a time would come when Americans and more and more Europeans can take for granted that 'what I mean by democracy' must mean both freedom and popular government – what else? But the tension remains, though we may now call what we have some doubts about populism rather than democracy. It became almost a catchphrase in

France when anyone uttered a portentous banality to say, '*Comme disait M. de Tocqueville*'. So be it. It is no mean achievement to get difficult truths accepted as banal. I began my *In Defence of Politics* by saying that I wanted 'to make some platitudes pregnant'. I still do.

Chapter 5
Democracy and populism

Fourscore and seven years ago our fathers brought forth on this continent , a new nation, conceived in Liberty, and dedicated to the proposition that all men are created equal. Now we are engaged in a great civil war, testing whether that nation or any nation so conceived and so dedicated, can long endure ... It is for us the living ... to be here dedicated to the great task remaining before us ... that this nation, under God, shall have a new birth of freedom – and that government of the people, by the people, for the people, shall not perish from the earth.

> (Abraham Lincoln at Gettysburg, November 1863)

To the BELOVED REPUBLIC under whose equal laws I am made the peer of any man, although denied equality by my native land, I DEDICATE THIS BOOK with an intensity of gratitude and admiration which the native-born citizen can neither feel nor understand.

> (Andrew Carnegie, *Triumphant Democracy:*
> *Fifty Years' March of the Republic*, 1887)

This passage in the Gettysburg address, dedicating a national cemetery on the recent battleground – the civil war still not over – attempts to unify and sanctify in the American political mind the ideas of liberty contained in the Declaration of Independence and the broad majoritarian democratic ideas

8. Abraham Lincoln (1809–65) study by Matthew Brady, 1863.

'of the people, by the people'. Lincoln deliberately gave the Declaration a moral priority over the constitution which, after all, made no reference to equality and tolerated slavery. Anti-abolitionist Unionists angrily protested that the President in this speech to the people was bypassing the constitution as he had done in the emancipation proclamation. But war is sometimes an accelerator of social change and can strengthen shared values. When the Chief Justice had protested at the beginning of the war at Lincoln nationalizing the telegraphs by presidential decree, Lincoln had remarked that Taney should send his man round to talk to his man, after the war. Democracies have to defend themselves.

By the third quarter of the 19th century the example of the United States, indeed its very existence, showed that democracy was possible, just this blend of individual liberty and popular power, even in a country of continental scale, no longer cities with extended hinterlands. When the civil war broke out conservative opinion all over Europe had said 'told you so', democracy would result in anarchy – as the study of the classics and the French Revolution had taught them. But the victory of the north, the emancipation of the slaves, the economic strength of northern industry, the patriotism of the citizen armies, and the speeches of Lincoln gave them an answer. The title of Carnegie's book would certainly remind them that a democratic capitalist society had triumphed over the agrarian 'cottonocracy' of the plantation owners.

As the immigrant ships came into New York harbour, the Statue of Liberty was soon to greet them, and inscribed upon it:

> Give me your tired, your poor
> Your huddled masses yearning to be free
> The wretched refuse of your teeming short,
> Send these, the homeless, tempest-tossed to me.
> I lift my lamp beside the golden door.

Carnegie was right. His native land had still denied him the vote when he had migrated to 'the land of the free' and his father, indeed, had been imprisoned in Scotland as a Chartist agitator, demanding 'one man one vote', annual parliaments, and the secret ballot. The United States embodied the principle of democracy, just as for much of the 20th century Russia was to embody the principle of Communist socialism. Small wonder that the very teaching of American history was forbidden in both the 19th-century Habsburg and Romanov empires.

Home truths

At that time no one could sensibly describe the British system of parliamentary government as democratic. The cult of the gentleman ruled, not that of the common man. Carnegie knew his Robert Burns:

> We see yon birkie ca'd a lord
>   Wha struts and stares, and a'that,
> Though hundreds worship at his word,
>   He's but a coof for a' that,
> His ribannd, star and a' that,
>   The man of independant mind,
> He looks and laughs at a' that.

But satire and democratic abuse did not make the growth of the franchise in Britain other than deliberately and spectacularly slow. Despite strong popular agitation, the 1832 Reform Act had no whiff whatever of democracy about it: it put the old property franchises on a uniform and more rational basis, only increasing the electorate from about 435,000 to some 652,000. Hegel called the British constitution after 1832 'the furthest advance in world history of the principle of freedom'. The Reform Act of 1867 was a response to working-class agitation and was of far greater consequence than that of 1832, but the new property and rent qualifications aimed to enfranchise only skilled workers. By 1869 about a third of adult males were entitled to vote, which the 1884 Act raised to about 40%. Neither Gladstone nor Disraeli believed in a fully democratic franchise, Gladstone the moralist and gradualist, Disraeli the tolerant opportunist. But if the 1867 Reform Act was not fully democratic, it did create such large numbers of new voters that the party system had to spread out of Westminster and, for the first time ever, organize and campaign nationally. Party leaders had both to show their faces in the country and endure far too many visits from power-brokers with uncouth accents from Birmingham, Sheffield, Manchester, and the northern industrial cities. Universal suffrage to include even women, after the bitter debates and the civil disobedience campaigns of the Suffragettes, came only by nervous stages, not until the Representation of the People Acts of 1918 and 1928. The exigencies of war, not sweet reason, changed parliamentary opinion. Democratic practices were common in the growing trade union and Labour movements, but not in parliament or in parliamentary elections.

Within the British Liberal Party a debate grew about whether the constitution should be more *democratic* – as Lloyd George argued in the 1900s, but his leader, Asquith, thought it quite democratic enough already, thank you. Was there not a free press, freedom of speech, and toleration by the local magistrates of mass meetings? 'The platform' had grown more rapidly than the franchise.

Conservative leaders repeated many of the old arguments about the dangers of democracy, but gradually qualifiers slipped in front of that damned 'D' word – the dangers of 'unbridled', 'ill-informed', 'excessive', or 'uneducated' democracy. And a figure like Joseph Chamberlain had sublime confidence, as had Disraeli before him, that the people could be 'managed'. Joe Chamberlain had had his power base in 'the Birmingham caucus' (a term imported from American politics), but had broken from the Liberal Party over Gladstone's Home Rule for Ireland Bill of 1886, bringing down the

THE TWO AUGURS.

9. Mr Punch sees Gladstone and Disraeli as noble Romans anxious to foresee the future of politics.

government and allying his followers as Unionists with the Conservatives. He had the art of managing the new electorate in the names of king and country, imperial patriotism, free trade, or else empire preferences in tariffs – whichever guaranteed 'cheap food for the masses'.

'Democracy' was not a term to rally the country. The British system was not to be described as democratic even in scholarly books. It first began to be called 'democratic' in the press, and quite often in parliament in the middle of 1916 when the ghastly losses on the Somme called for some justification about 'what we are fighting for' greater than 'king and country', a *sluaghghairm* or rallying cry more appealing to factory workers and the conscript squaddies, especially those on the Celtic fringe. And when Woodrow Wilson brought the United States into the war, it became a war 'to save democracy', official – even if Congress lost interest afterwards in any international dimension of democracy, rejecting Wilson's plea to sign up to the League of Nations into which he had poured his hopes and last energies. The leaders of the post-war Labour Party, which was anxious to distance itself from Soviet Communism, showed more interest in gaining power for the sake of 'the people', in using the existing parliamentary system, than in changing it in democratic directions, still less socialist. There was tension in the Labour movement, however. At that time 'municipal socialism' was strong and was, like the unions and co-operative societies, democratic in how decisions were made as well as in their egalitarian aims. There were two theories of democratic socialism: one that it should build up from the roots of society, quasi-autonomous small groups, local unions, and local government, and the other that central power must be gained in Whitehall through Westminster for the benefit of the people – the theory of the Fabians, the Webbs, and today of New Labour (albeit with a new image of 'the people').

Walter Bagehot's famous *The English Constitution* (1867) used to be read as an objective and descriptive work in a new genre of realism – much like Manet's *Déjeuner sur l'herbe* compared to the paintings of the Academy, as when Bagehot said in his chapter on the monarchy, 'it is nice to trace how the actions of a retired widow and an unemployed youth become of such importance'. But not just realism. The book was a polemic on the Reform Bill controversies of 1867. He was a Liberal warning of the dangers of democracy but counselling how they could be averted by many devices: 'The use of the Queen, in a dignified capacity, is incalculable' – the very first sentence of that chapter. In the introduction to the book's second edition of 1872 he comes clean and clear, in case people had missed the subtext:

> In plain English, what I fear is that both our political parties will bid for the support of the working man; that both of them will promise to do as he likes if he will only tell them what it is . . . I can conceive of nothing more corrupting or worse for a set of poor ignorant people than that two combinations of well-taught and rich men should constantly offer to defer to their decision, and compete for the office of executing it. *Vox populi* will be *Vox diaboli* if it is worked in that manner.

His greatest fear, he continued, was a permanent 'political combination of the lower classes . . . now that so many of them have the suffrage . . . the supremacy of ignorance over instruction and of numbers over knowledge'. Why his fears proved exaggerated, even with the growth of the trade union movement and the Labour Party, is another story. But its main theme might be that the grandees of both the Tory Party and Liberal Party had to learn to play the demagogue, like the Roman patricians whose fears Bagehot echoes with his scorn for the tag, *Vox populi, vox dei*. When Gladstone came back from retirement (yet again) to demand British intervention against Turkey over the Armenian atrocities, he spoke in the famous Midlothian campaign *from the back of railway trains* and, moreover, spoke in other Members' constituencies, creating immediate fear that British politics was becoming American.

Populism

The mass franchise in the USA (brushing aside, of course, women and the blacks) spread a style of politics which, if certainly not wholly new, broke from the manner of careful reasoned argument, as if actually trying to persuade, that had been the style of 'citizen literature' of the early republic or, indeed, of the debates over slavery and secession; and the style of parliamentary debates in Great Britain. That older style had been appropriate to a smaller political class, often bound together by friendship, even family connection, at the least by social acquaintance and common codes of behaviour. But to address a mass meeting or appeal to a mass franchise, the power to comprehend and stir common emotions was needed. The greatest art was plain speaking, to combine simple language with common sense and wisdom, as did Lincoln – much criticized at the time for the homely, undignified language of his most lasting and famous speeches. But the blackest art could be called, and was, 'rabble-rousing'.

Populism has come to mean many things, but I see it as a style of politics and rhetoric that seeks to arouse a majority, or at least what their leaders passionately believe is a majority (like 'moral majority' today, who are plainly a minority), who are, have been, or think themselves to be outside the polity, scorned and despised by an educated establishment. If the civilized debates of the upper crust had been honed in court houses and in elected assemblies, the skills of the populist orator had most often been honed in, or by the example of, the evangelical pulpits and the revival meetings. Nowadays we can too easily forget the influence of the pulpit, at least in Britain. The pulpits of the American Revolution reached more people and were probably at least as influential as the debates in the town meetings or among the few in the legislatures. In England the first mass meetings of ordinary people were in the Wesleyan revival. Still earlier in Scotland the Covenanters had met similarly in fields or on hillsides, but were suppressed; so not until the Chartist and then the Labour movement, two centuries later, did agitational meetings take place in public buildings or town squares.

In the United States what we now call 'populism' or 'populist democracy' took the form of rural interests against the cities. For that was where most of Jefferson and Jackson's 'plain people' were. Not until the 1930s did a majority of Americans live in towns of over 3,000 inhabitants. The historian Richard Hofstadter found that the peculiar character of American populism 'derives in great part from the American tradition of entrepreneurial radicalism'. Elsewhere populism drew upon a peasantry tied to the land as part of the ownership by an aristocracy or local grandees of large estates, as in tsarist Russia and even today in South America and India. But American farmers, however small their farm, however poor, were freeholders and strident individualists; yet they could be roused to collective action by a sense of common grievances. The common enemies were invariably 'the government' (the 'citizen militias' of today hate government), the bankers, the railroad companies, the capitalist system – and somehow all too often the Catholic Church, the Jews, and the blacks shared the blame for the sad lot of the poor farmer (what Hofstadter called, in the title of a book, *The Paranoid Style in American Politics*). But if they felt persecuted, it was because they often were. The patent remedies they chose were often crazily simplistic and inappropriate to their sufferings. The populist orator William Jennings Bryan swept the Democratic Party convention of 1896 with his 'cross of gold' speech, demanding that silver be restored alongside 'crucifying gold' as the national currency. Endorsed as Democratic presidential candidate, also with the support of the People's Party, he gained an impressive 6,502,925 votes as against McKinley's 7,104,779. The greatest triumph of populism as a national movement was Prohibition, the 18th amendment of the constitution of 1919. But some of the targets and tactics of 'the moral majority' today are of this kind. There's no reasoning with the plain people about the literal truth of the Bible, and their cries can be heard by Presidents.

Hofstadter quoted a pamphleteer in Iowa in 1893 who just about summed it up:

> Whenever, in a populous Nation, agricultural pursuits become of secondary importance as a means of acquiring wealth, it may be set down as certain that the callings which have risen above it are operating under some *artificial* stimulus which is *abnormal and unjust*.

This could almost be Rousseau again: the artificial threatens the natural, and it is one incident in the perennial struggle between the values of the countryside and nature, those of the cities, and induced, artificial learning. But there is another version of this, of course: that it is the countryside that is the seat of 'rural superstition' (as Machiavelli said in Europe and Henry Mencken said in America) and the recruiting ground for reactionary armies hostile or indifferent to the quibbling values of free citizens. Perhaps we should laugh at Schiller's panic that began the Romantic movement when he heard that there was a *factory* in Swabia; and not forget that Blake's 'dark satanic mills', dark as they were, had something to do with the huge general increase in standard of living of industrial countries which has something to do with an effective democracy.

Capitalist democracy and liberalism

By 1886, when that verse appeared on the newly erected Statue of Liberty, the democratic self-identity of the United States was being reimagined. Some would continue to say, as the newspaper editor Horace Greeley intoned, 'Go West, young man, go West', but working on the land was beginning to lose its attraction to immigrants and the native-born alike – except the 'get rich quick' allure of the gold rush, or more like the 'California or bust!' written on the wagons, then 'Busted'. From *Log Cabin to White House* was a popular book that came to name a whole genre of popular literature, but the later versions had to become, as it were, 'from tenement to boardroom'. The early Republican ideal of the yeoman farmer was giving way to the virtues of urban capitalism and concern for, or fear of, the urban masses. Something of what became the (unsuccessful) 'populist revolt' in American politics was triggered by loss of esteem as well as by poverty, the great agricultural depression, and growing indebtedness to the banks. Urban capitalism had to find a democratic legitimation.

This legitimation was found both in popular literature and in social theory. At the very time of the great 'robber barons', the post-civil war generation of railroad and steel tycoons and bankers too (Pierpoint Morgan was reputed to have said to President Cleveland, 'what's the constitution between friends?' – nowadays the oilmen and the mining interests are more discreet), a popular literature emerged called 'success novels'. Perhaps the most famous was Horatio Alger's *From Rags to Riches*. The slogan of democratic capitalism became 'There is room for all at the top'. Alger strove to rationalize this falsehood (and Orwell, long after, mocked the ethics of the competitive society by remarking that 'the trouble with competitions is that someone has to win'). In *Luke Larkin's Luck*, Luke is a poor orphan on the streets. But he manfully resists joining a street gang headed, of course, by a Mickey McGuire, and he honestly and sensibly puts into a savings bank a dime of every dollar he earns by watching gentlemen's horses and running errands. Alger tells us that Mickey McGuire was 'a democrat in the worst sense', he 'threatened respectable voters on election day' (presumably paid by Tammany Hall), and in general was 'loud and violent in his manners with no respect for his betters'. Luke Larkin, however, was 'a democrat in the finest sense . . . a help to his fellows' and he respected the law, worked hard and honestly, and in what spare time he has he visits a free library seeking to improve himself. But there is the obvious problem. There is not room for everyone at the top. However, Luke happens to walk by the East River when a millionaire's daughter falls in, and he rescues her at the risk of his life. Or in other novels other Lukes stop teams of stampeding horses saving other millionaires' daughters in driverless carriages. In each case the hero is given a job in the counting house and swiftly rises up, sometimes marrying that daughter. Alger ruminates, 'there has been some luck about it, I admit', but goes on to claim that but for Luke's prior virtue luck would not have struck and also that but for that virtue he could not have done so well in the job offered; and notice that he wanted a job as a reward not a fistful of dollars. Hard work, virtue, and a bit of luck became what was actually called 'the democratic gospel of wealth'. It *was* democratic because even if there was not room for all at the top, the idea was that anybody could get to the top regardless of social class. Most preachers of the day (and many today too) took the view that riches are a heavenly reward for virtue, albeit the rich had a duty to practise philanthropy, to be charitable – to their own best judgement.

The legitimation of democratic capitalism in theory can be seen in the tremendous sales and popularity in the USA, more so than in the prophet's own country, of Herbert Spencer's *Man versus the State*. His sociology was a potent blend of belief in inevitable progress, 'social Darwinism' (a variant of Thomas Huxley's law of nature, 'the survival of the fittest'), and extreme *laissez-faire*, free-market theory. He argued that society was a *system* that would achieve a natural equilibrium if the state did not interfere: every attempt at reform nearly always upset this equilibrium and only substituted one evil for another. If at times society did appear 'red in tooth and claw', this was inevitable because evolutionary progress was weeding out the unfit from the fit. This doctrine had a small army of both academic and popularizing authors. It was welcomed by the men of new wealth because they did have problems not with state ownership, scarcely with socialism (though some of them feared it beyond reason and local cause), but with a great deal of Congressional regulation of canals, railroads, public utilities, company law, and the use of public lands. These regulations were often a response to local political pressures; and the regulators were then associated with the paternalist mentality of old wealth and an old ruling elite, no longer anti-democratic in Tocqueville's sense, certainly not anti-capitalist, but inclined to interfere too much in a pragmatic way, in a responsible way as they saw it, with free enterprise. The word 'liberal' began to be attached to them, irrespective of whether their political affiliation, which largely depended on which section of the country they lived in, was Republican or Democrat.

Two usages of 'liberalism' had emerged and were to stay, on both side of the water. One was virtually synonymous with *laissez-faire* capitalism and free-market economics. But the other had a more political and cultural stress. Individual liberty must be maximized, but the liberties of all could be limited by the unbridled liberties of a few. Therefore some regulatory frameworks had to be imposed – anti-trust legislation became the paradigm case. But also civil liberties needed special protection against both abuses of free enterprise and abuses of the democratic franchise: the rule of law (the constitution, especially the Bill of Rights, and the federal courts) must put limits on individualism. The National Parks movement of the 1900s shows that there were cultural values in this liberalism willing to take on even the mining, railroad, and soon the oil interest on the wilder side of capitalism – with some successes.

Capitalist populism

Carnegie's *Triumphant Democracy* showed the tensions both between these two types of liberalism and between each and individualism. He took the survival of the fittest so literally that he faced the problem of the accumulation of capital. The self-made man was the democratic hero, but what should he do with his wealth? He polemicized against 'the rich man's son'. He had not earned it. Inherited wealth corrupts the virtue needed for earning great wealth and for enjoying its possession. 'Cursed be the man who dies rich,' he said. Evolution demands that the millionaire gives away his money. It had also demanded, of course, that he had let his managers send in the armed Pinkerton men by the barge-load to break, most bloodily, a determined and desperate strike at his Bethlehem Steel Works. But the Carnegie Foundation for World Peace was real and well funded. Carnegie believed like all liberals, until 1914, that the new global economy and the lowering of tariff barriers would ensure peace among capitalist nations and the withering away of war.

But the problem remained of how to spend domestically without interfering with the evolutionary process. Herbert Spencer had lectured at a great dinner in his honour by the money men of New York on the thoughtless iniquity of even putting a dime in a beggar's cup. Small wonder, he intoned, that the beggar spent that dime on beer or tobacco and not in smartening-up to look for work. Relief of the poor did but perpetuate those unfit for progress. So how to help people to help themselves without giving them money? The answer suddenly became as obvious to Carnegie as it had long been to Mill – education, or in Carnegie's case more specifically the free public library. And he spread them not merely in America but throughout his native Scotland (ruining, incidentally, several small burghs because the only condition on the gift of a building was to fill it with books, and the smallest of the templates on offer was often too large). Mr Dooley, the Chicago-Irish humorist, had Carnegie's butler telling him that a tramp was at the door asking for a glass of milk and a bread roll. 'No, do not pauperise that poor man further. Give him a library.' Carnegie also bought up English and Scottish provincial newspapers to run them in Gladstone's and the Liberal Party's interest. A gross intrusion into another country's politics with a favour-seeking motive? Far from it. He was no Murdoch and had no need to seek favours from Gladstone. He sought only to speed up the inevitable evolutionary process of democracy in which Britain was somewhat behind America.

There was, of course, another breed of urban populist, an equally strange product of urban capitalist democracy, who did give out a little milk, some bread rolls, and a lot of jobs: the new city political machines of the Irish immigrants, later the Italians too. Alger's Mickey McGuires would work for them and did, indeed, often intimidate respectable voters from going to the polls. But the bosses of Tammany Hall and the like in other cities were of and for their people, although Lincoln's 'by the people' got no look in. A Tammany *sachem* or lieutenant of Mayor Richard Croker, one George Washington Plunkitt, famously philosophized that 'silk stocking principles are all very well, but they don't get you far in the 14th precinct' where it was also 'no use talking Shakespeare'. But of course this kind of affable tolerance of electoral corruption, so long as done by our people, has not entirely vanished and spreads far beyond the big cities, at times even determining the results of presidential elections themselves.

So liberal democracy had different modes in the USA but the overall dominating ideology was liberalism. There was no real Conservative tradition in European terms, nor socialism neither. Many books have been written about both but neither had any lasting effect on either the politics or the culture. This is why I have spent so much space on democracy in the USA, because there the constitutional and individualist strengths and the populist weaknesses are still

10. **Woodrow Wilson meeting Congressmen, imagined by Max Beerbohm.**

most vivid to the whole world in contrast to the more ideological political and class-cultural divisions of the old world. Louis Hartz wrote in *The Liberal Tradition in America* that 'the reality of atomistic social freedom is the master assumption of American political thought'; and argued that *the tradition* was liberal. This is only a paradox to Europeans, to whom tradition has been conservative and who, to this day, have some discomfort or confusion, whatever we call ourselves, about the very concept of democracy, even liberal democracy. H. G. Wells in a thoughtful travel book of 1906, *The Future in America*, said:

> the American community ... does not correspond to an entire European community at all, but only to the middle masses of it, to the trading and manufacturing class ... It is the central part of the European organism without either the dreaming head or the subjugated feet ... Essentially America is a middle class become a community and so its essential problems are those of a modern individualistic society, stark and clear, unhampered and unilluminated by any feudal traditions either at its crest or at its base.

Contemporary populism

To move into the world of today with just one rather interesting example of populism. Two years ago the editor of the London Sunday tabloid *News of the World* decided to publish the addresses of paedophiles released from prison. And at the same time the *Big Brother* television programmes were playing on Channel Four. In that game the viewers could vote who was to be chucked out one by one each week from the closed community, televised in their every moment – well, not quite, until only the prizewinner was left. So one could surf easily from the angry mob scenes in Portsmouth outside the home of an alleged released paedophile to those outside the *Big Brother* studio when Caroline – wasn't it? – was released or kicked out. The one mob was, of course, ugly, full of hate, potentially violent, while the other was facetiously high-spirited when they screamed, 'we hate Nick'. One for real and one for play, but both were mobs.

Hannah Arendt in her *Origins of Totalitarianism* distinguished between 'the people' and 'the mob'. The people seek for effective representation politically, whereas the mob hates society from which it has been excluded. Interestingly she called them a residue of *all* classes (the social class and occupations of arrested football hooligans is indeed more mixed than many would expect). The mob, she argued, are highly individualistic, all for number one, as it were; unless a charismatic leader emerges to legitimize their sense of being outside society, to bond their common hatreds for longer than spasmodic riots. Our two mobs are excluded from society in rather different ways, of course: the mob on the run-down Paulsgrove housing estate are, by many measures of social deprivation, objectively excluded; whereas the mob on the factoid studio set are subjectively excluded; they cheerfully exclude themselves from conventional ideas of seriousness and social responsibility. Let us call the two the full-of-hate mob and the empty mob.

So Channel Four had, indeed, created or adapted a brilliant entertainment for the empty mob, a cunning synthesis of game show and debased, dumbed-down documentary which impels, for at least four reasons, some serious attention as to how populism can thrive in a liberal-democratic culture. First, it creates the illusion of naturalism. Nearly all tele-dramas, not just the soaps, are for us watching others like ourselves doing recognizable things; very little imagination, fantasy, or magic realism; even if the frequency of murder, rape, other violent crimes, and even sex on first sight are statistically abnormal. They close down not broaden imaginative horizons. But most of us know that all that is made up. A caution, however: I remember having to tell a partner's 11-year-old foster child that the cowboys and Indians we were watching on the box were not really getting killed. She had asked me why anyone took on the job. This is the twilight zone of the factoids that can fool or confuse even adults – those movies that *know* why Kennedy was killed or reconstruct the judicial murder of a Saudi royal princess. We are too often in the world of confusion between journalism and entertainment. Channel Four made fatuous claims that *Big Brother* was serious reporting on how people react under pressure. Considering how heavily the surveillance film has to be cut and edited, and how aware the happy family is that they may be on camera, this is (in Bentham's words) nonsense on stilts.

Secondly, *Big Brother* gave the viewers sentencing power: the illusion of democratic participation and of popular power, happily in this case an illusion – unlike being given the addresses of alleged paedophiles. 'Crucify him, crucify him!' Not merely the tabloids feed this mentality, but increasingly the BBC. The *Today* programme will ask a relative of a victim how the perpetrator should be punished; or, with judicious economy, interview one ordinary person to gain, all too often, a snap, ignorant, prejudiced opinion as if representative of 'the people'; well, at least an *authentic* voice, a magic word that links populism high and low, in art as well as in journalism and sometimes government.

Thirdly, *Big Brother* attracted a huge mob to come and watch on the ground the expulsions from the anti-Paradise of those they had voted out. Davina, the presenter, dashed through them, like a frenzied post-modernist Anglo-Saxon messenger in *Alice*, inciting and feeding their lines, but all scripted, of course, unlike the mob leaders in Portsmouth. *She* was the apt embodiment of clamorous triviality or the purity of purposelessness. Not quite the Greek goddess Demokratia. And the empty mob could then go home and look for themselves on video playing at being a full-of-hate mob. Such is modern reality.

Fourthly, *Big Brother* stood Orwell's metaphor on its head. If any of the empty mob were to read *Nineteen Eighty-Four*, disappointment would be in store. Orwell's Airstrip One was under a totalitarian dictatorship. The telescreen was emphatically not for entertainment. Here he missed what was growing under his nose. But screens today *are* used for surveillance, even if now mainly for entertainment. The programme *Big Brother* pretended to be the voice of the people, or the empty mob. Well, we are a democracy, aren't we? Why can't the people have what they want? Even if a kind of democratic dictatorship, or what Tocqueville called the tyranny of the majority? No need for knowledge, reasoned discussion, recourse to authorities and experience. That is what populists call elitism. We don't want any of that. But just to point out that the case for populism replacing a construct of society based on good government, representative democracy, and reasoned debate, this would be stronger if those in TV and the tabloids who hide behind public opinion, while seeking to stir it to commercial advantage, really did make serious attempts to ascertain what it is – not just viewing figures, emails, readers' letters, and, of course, an editor's intuition. But professional in-depth public opinion surveys are expensive. Easier and cheaper to send a reporter out to find a colourful and articulate individual. Populist trendies are shocked to be reminded of Beatrice Webb's deflating aphorism that democracy is not the multiplication of ignorant opinions. But pause a moment. Surely reasoning, liberty, and human rights must limit or interact with the will of the majority? Take the issue of capital punishment, for instance.

Orwell's own version in *Nineteen Eighty-Four* of Big Brother's method of domination had some similarity to the world of sitcoms, game shows, and the prize inanities of *Big Brother*. Party members were tightly controlled, but the inner party made no attempt to turn the proles from spasmodic mob into party members. They are simply depoliticized by cultural debasement, dumbing down, kept even from thinking of demanding fair shares. The Minitrue, remember, had a special department for the proles:

Here were produced rubbishy newspapers containing almost nothing except sport, crime and astrology, sensational five-cent novelettes, films oozing with sex, and sentimental songs which were composed entirely by mechanical means on a special kind of kaleidoscope known as a versificator. There was even a whole sub-section; *Pornosec* engaged in producing the lowest kinds of pornography.

This was not satire of Stalin's and Hitler's regimes; both those gentlemen were conventionally prudish and tried hard to indoctrinate and mobilize the masses. Orwell's was savage satire of Britain's popular press: it was a gross, Swiftian exaggeration or caricature, fed by his sardonic pessimism. Only one newspaper fitted the bill back then – the *News of the World*.

Orwell was perfectly serious in arguing that capitalism, faced with an at least formally literate and free electorate, can only maintain a system of gross inequalities and inequities of wealth by means of cultural debasement, a deliberate underuse of the resources and potential of literacy. Did he know of Habermas and the Frankfurt school of neo-Marxism? They argued just this. I doubt it. Old George probably worked it out for himself. The editor who stirred the full-of-hate mob may have thought she understood the common people instinctively or she may just have been selling newspapers. But she certainly stirred a mob reaction in populist manner on an issue that needs sensitive and informed leadership and serious democratic debate, careful and caring thought, not instinctive and precipitate action. Happily some voices of reason in the media began to remind us that there were only five child murders the previous year compared to hundreds of deaths on the roads and that 98% of recorded child abuse is within families. While tabloid reports of cases of child abuse, murder, welfare scroungers, incompetent doctors, etc. are usually well-researched and true (for fear of libel if they got it wrong), they are most often numerically insignificant and rarely offer or seek to find aggregate or comparative figures. Panics make news, comparative statistics are boring and demanding – elitist.

Throughout this small but illustrative incident, leading politicians talked far more strongly and more often of the need for new laws (offering no clear reasons except that some newspapers were demanding them) than they did in rebuke of the vigilantes. Baldwin rebuked Beaverbrook in 1936 for exercising 'power without responsibility; the prerogative of the harlot throughout the ages'. Could one imagine a modern prime minister or president speaking like this to a Murdoch? But Baldwin lived in elitist not populist days. Or is it more a matter of political courage, to appeal to the best instincts of people, not the worst? And perhaps rather than new laws, staffing levels and training in local support services are part of such problems, just as the root of the problems of poor education and lawlessness in those sad estates are largely economic (surely both socialists and free-marketeers would agree?). But we do not care to spend individually for what collectively we need. A politics of competitive tax-cutting has been practised. There must be limits to individualism. Orwell understood the difference between what the public is interested in, and the public interest. That is why he wrote that book whose warning has been treated with cynical contempt and itself appropriated in the *Big Brother* programme as prolefeed. There must be some better democratic, not simply populist, way of deciding matters. The populist mode of democracy is a politics of arousal more than of reason, but also a politics of diversion from serious concerns that need settling in either a liberal democratic or a civic republican manner.

Chapter 6
The conditions of modern democracy

The world must be made safe for democracy.
> (Woodrow Wilson, address to Congress, 2 April 1917)

There was an old man who supposed
That the street door was partially closed,
But some very large rats ate his coat and his hats
While that futile old gentleman dozed.

> (Edward Lear)

When the American founding fathers said that 'all government rests on the consent of the people' they were either plain wrong or assuming that it *should* do so; and they assumed that when it did so the people would always be benign. They believed that what they had already could one day become universal. Already they were a confederacy of states with some forms of representative assemblies, however limited their powers, of citizens who wished to be independent of arbitrary external rule. The effective rallying cry, 'no taxation without representation', was really part of a more general claim, 'no obedience without representation' or 'no laws other than made by our elected representatives'. This last claim is what Mill was to mean by *Representative Government* and what most people today would mean simply by democracy. But most people when prodded into thought, by conflicts of values and interests or perhaps by little books, would want to add that even democratically made laws must respect individual liberties and some acceptable formulation of human rights. All government did not rest upon consent, except in the clear but almost trivial sense that even a war lord if he is to sleep must have trust in his guards, some cocoon of willing or induced consent. But in the modern industrial and globalizing world all governments seeking to manage such social transformation need mass consent – which is why so many military dictatorships claim to be democratic and, in the primal sense of the term, are democratic, depend on an active mass support in a way that no despot or autocrat in older peasant societies needed to.

So now I am grappling with a basic misunderstanding. Strictly speaking I am writing about democracy in a book so titled, but most readers will expect 'democracy' to be synonymous with good government or political justice in general. The term is commonly used for what we value most highly or are supposed to value, rather than as an important element in good government. Good government should be democratic, in both an institutional and a social sense, but also include individual liberties, human rights, economic progress, and social justice – which is something more than equality of political rights. If this sounds like Aristotle again, that democracy is a necessary element in good government but neither the ideal nor the form of the whole, so it is. That little tale about 'populism' should show that the democratic spirit can get out of hand. I have heard well-meaning people demand that schools should be democratic. That is, alas, Rousseau-like nonsense: that innocence is superior to knowledge, or is itself a form of knowledge. But I have argued strongly elsewhere that schools should be *more* democratic than they commonly are. I see citizenship education as a democratic impulse, but a democratic school is a contradiction in terms. It is easier to say when a government or any other form of authority is acting undemocratically than to say when it is acting *truly* democratically, except in the basic and minimal sense that it governs in a democratic context: faces periodic re-election and abides by the results, has to make known its decisions (even sometimes how it reaches its decisions), and allows public criticism

11. Christabel Pankhurst exhorting a suffragette meeting in Trafalgar Square to surround the House of Commons, 11 October, 1908.

in the media. My understanding of what most people mean by democracy is what the Greeks meant by 'polity' or simply political rule, a system that allows for peaceable compromises to be made between ever-present conflicts of values and of interests. That is why I wrote an *In Defence of Politics* and not an 'In Defence of Democracy'; so two cheers for democracy, not three.

The conditions of modern democracy

But enough on the ambiguities and 'the dangers of democracy'. I may begin to sound anti-democratic. Let me yield to popular usage, with a slight compromise, and ask what the conditions for a *modern* democracy are, even if I might pedantically prefer to say 'political regimes' or even 'republican government'; for it is forms of government that constitute the real question at issue.

One can be more precise than is often thought to be the case about the conditions for modern democracy if one thinks historically and comparatively about the key factors conditioning but never fully determining forms of government. Any academic worth her or his salt will have a different listing of factors set in a different 'conceptual framework' with which to stimulate their students or torment them with neologisms. But I see something like these factors as important for all forms of government: the role of the inhabitants, official doctrines, typical social structure, the nature of the elite, typical institutions of government, type of economy, theories of property, attitudes to law, attitudes to knowledge, diffusion of information, attitudes to politics.

Let us see the form modern democracy takes for each of these, and sometimes contrasts with autocratic and even totalitarian forms may be helpful.

- *Role of the inhabitants.* Voluntary and individual participation is encouraged in modern democracies, but not compulsory. A person is free to act as a citizen or not, hence a discriminatory kind of loyalty. Only in time of war can the state mobilize all its inhabitants, otherwise people are free to move backward and forward between public and private life. To the liberal, just laws allow a maximization of private and commercial life; to the republican, a state is weak and private life incomplete without a high degree of civil participation. The contrast with autocracies is marked: they thrive on passive obedience and social deference ('let sleeping dogs lie'); and with would-be totalitarian regimes that need to mobilize their inhabitants for social transformation.
- *Official doctrines.* Allegiance in democracies is demanded and given by popular consent and on utilitarian and secular grounds: the state must demonstrate practical benefits in the here and now and not the hereafter. If authority is not truly a contract between rulers and ruled, yet commonly a contractarian language is spoken, as if rights depend upon duties. There is tolerance of diverse doctrines, so long as the behaviour which may follow does not directly threaten public

order or the safety of the state. In most autocracies allegiance is a religious duty, the state and its rulers being seen as part of a divine order. In modern would-be totalitarian states allegiance is owed to an ideology claiming to be comprehensive and prophetic of the course of history, and even inner reservations threaten the safety of the state.

- *Typical social structure.* All the ancient and modern authorities agree that a large middle class is essential (which is partly why Marxists used to reject modern democracy as a 'capitalist, bourgeois sham'). Extremes of wealth in the hands of a few can threaten democratic processes, and extremes of poverty remove people from the normal polity and can threaten order. What is extreme is, however, always politically contestable. 'Middle class' need not mean other clear classes. The post-Marxist idea of a classless society is that of a middle class or bourgeois classlessness – the American, Australian, Swedish, Dutch, post-war German, and Blairite or New Labour ideal, even if reality lags behind. Autocracies have highly stratified class or caste systems. Totalitarian regimes aim to be egalitarian but in fact develop a class system based on political and bureaucratic office-holding.
- *Nature of the elite.* Usually a fairly stable political class enjoying some prestige, but sharing status with business, intellectual, and social elites, and open and penetrable to varying extents by candidates from educational institutions partly designed to recruit talent and encourage mobility. The extent of mobility and openness is perpetually debatable, both for intention and result; and the relative prestige of the political elite now seems in or in danger of decline. In autocracies the elite is usually self-perpetuating and exclusive, and in totalitarian regimes it is in theory a meritocracy based on perfect social mobility but in practice more often a self-perpetuating inner party served by a relatively large and more genuinely meritocratic outer party.
- *Typical institutions of government.* The parliament, the assembly,

the congress, all elective, debating in public and reported, and in a multi-party system. Nearly always there is some devolution of powers to or continuation of old powers in local or regional governments. Systems of elections are almost infinitely variable and contestable. (In Britain 'first past the post' can be called undemocratic, certainly unrepresentative; but the answer is then that to ask 'is it democratic?' is the wrong question; the right one is then said to be 'does it contribute to clear, good, firm government?') In autocracies the court or the palace comprise a visible, awe-inspiring, and usually militarily defensible society within a society. There may be internal politics within the palace walls, but not in public. There may be rival courts for short periods of time – 'Come ye not to Court?' 'To whose Court, to the King's Court or to Hampton Court?' The typical institution in a totalitarian state is the single party.

- *Type of economy.* A market or capitalist economy in origin, theory, and ethos, but in reality usually a mixed economy, sometimes consciously and decidedly so, as in social democratic or democratic socialist regimes. Most autocracies (and military governments) are in agrarian societies. Attempts to industrialize either lead to democratization as power is spread and criticism is needed, or to concentrations of power as if towards totalitarianism but usually resulting in chronic economic and political instability. The true totalitarian regimes were war economies, whether at war or not, rejecting 'mere' economic criteria.

- *Theories of property.* In a modern democracy the possession of property is still a mark of individual worthiness, originally moral worthiness but now more economic. Some believe that God distributes the prizes although not responsible for the handicaps on the runners; but even in secular terms wealth demands some justification. John Rawls rejects literal equality but argues that all inequalities need public justification in terms of benefits to others. Forms of property become ever more mobile and individual: from land as inheritance to land as purchase, from land to houses and workshops, then to joint-stock shares and to educationally acquired skills. So finally 'property' is mobile across national boundaries. In autocracies only land and treasure constitute property. In totalitarian regimes, in theory there is no personal property but invariably fruits, perks, and privileges of office.

- *Attitudes to law.* In autocracies law is either customary or the proclaimed will of the autocrat. In modern democracies law can be both customary and statutory, but new laws are made by a representative assembly or parliament. Law between individuals is largely a matter of contract but regulated by general rules by impartial judges not by personal favours or interventions as in autocracy. In totalitarian regimes law is interpreted by the general intentions of the ideology, not in the literal 'black letter' meaning of what is written down.

- *Attitudes to knowledge.* Again contrast makes modern democracy clearer. In autocracies knowledge is seen as a unified instrument of political power, part of the 'mysteries of power' or the unpublished 'reason of state' that is shared by the ruling elite but not to be questioned or debated publicly. Scientific and moral truths are confused and censorship is a necessary institution of state. In a modern democracy knowledge is seen as fragmented, related to problems not necessarily connected. Most moral truths are seen as relative in application, open to public debate, and distinct from scientific truths. There is official patronage of independent centres of learning and of the dissemination of knowledge. Knowledge has to be spread and remote from censorship if this kind of society is to work.

- *Diffusion of information.* Proclamations are typical of autocracies, newspapers of modern democracies. With no regular news, rumour and gossip become social institutions in autocracies, as does the spy as eavesdropper and the buffoon as safety valve or covert satirist. The growth of newspapers and their freedom from state control parallels the growth of the democratic franchise. Printed materials outpace oral communication and rumour as the source of public information. The effective working of democratic regimes comes to depend more and more on people having access to reasonably accurate information about how the state is run and on the state being able to assess public needs and reactions reasonably accurately. Hence the objective need for neutrality and objectivity in official publications, in stark comparison to all knowledge being seen as either propaganda or as secrets of state in totalitarian regimes.

- *Attitudes to politics*. In modern democracies politics is always tolerated and usually actively encouraged. Politics is recognized as a conciliatory public activity aimed at or involving compromise. In autocracies the regime is either above mere politics or politics is limited to the privacy of the palace, the court, or the inner party. In totalitarian regimes politics is denounced as a bourgeois sham and, like all compromises, either purely tactical or a symptom of social contradictions yet to be eradicated. 'Political parties exist to perpetuate problems,' said Goebbels, 'we exist to solve them.'

These very simple comparisons can show that while some basic problems and ambiguities in the history and understanding of 'democracy' have not disappeared (opinion versus knowledge, 'the dangers of the tyranny of the majority', populism, and the strength that mass support gives to some modern autocracies), yet features of great strength and importance emerge when we make comparisons with the worst rather than frustrate ourselves by comparisons with an ideal best. To point to only two features, and benefits: first, by comparison it is clear that autocracies are damaged when the truth is written and known about their systems of government. For closed elites all depend on some myths and deceptions about the way government is conducted. They are endangered if it is widely and openly said that they are not always wise and right, and that sometimes the ruling elite needs to conceal that they are systematically exploiting their people rather than caring for them. On the other hand, modern democracies can sustain truths being told about how the system works. Some argue that they are actually strengthened thereby because, unlike in autocracies, when the policies and plans of government are known and can be publicly criticized, they can be rectified or if necessary abandoned. Particular governments can be called to question, discredited, and even thrown out of office but the stability of the regime or the whole system of government is not usually threatened (unless public opinion is led to believe that all politicians are corrupt and self-serving, perhaps even that the very activity of politics is corrupt).

Secondly, comparison makes clear that open, transparent government and not merely freedom of information, its availability and circulation, can be as important as actual participation. Not for a moment to detract from the importance of participation (as an underpinning for moral education as well as a mechanism of democratic government), but on the scale of modern democracies there are severe limits to that direct participation which was at least the ideal of ancient democracies and city republics. So governments of large territories are restrained quite as much by knowing that people know what they are doing (something quite new in history), in other words by public opinion, as they are by people being directly participative. Also governments need to know whether they will be followed if they lead. Some legislation if it is to be successful needs a change in behaviour, not just respect for or fear of the law (say speed limits, public health campaigns, energy conservation, race relations, etc.). A wise American student of British politics, Samuel H. Beer, said that parliament was a device for 'mobilizing consent' as much as for representing existing consent. Good freedom of information legislation is likely to be as important in mobilizing an informed consent as improving the system of electoral representation.

A Japanese incident

The proposition that truths can and must be told about democratic systems but not about autocracies without endangering them can be illustrated from a cautionary tale told by Masao Maruyama, a Japanese political thinker and cultural historian. A certain Kono Hironaka was at first a traditionalist bitterly opposed to the planned modernization of Japan, but he later became founder and leader of the Japanese Liberal Party. He recounted in his memoir that his conversion took place through reading John Stuart Mill's *On Liberty* (the modernizers' choice of what to translate is interesting).

> I was riding on horseback when I first read this book. In a flash my entire way of thinking was revolutionised. Until then I had been under the influence of the Chinese Confucianists and of the Japanese classical scholars, and I had even been inclined to advocate an 'expel the barbarian' policy. Now all these earlier thoughts of mine, *excepting those concerned with loyalty and filial piety*, were smashed to smithereens. At the same moment I knew that it was human freedom and human rights that I must henceforth cherish above all else.

Maruyama pointed out with a sad anger that these two reservations proved fatal both to Japanese democracy and to a free 'political science' or critical study of politics, two entities that he saw as dependent on each other. 'Kono does not show the slightest awareness that the retention of this traditional morality might pose a problem for liberalism.' For 'filial piety' meant that no public criticism should be made of a member of one's clan (a very extended family), and 'loyalty' meant that when laws were passed by the parliament in the emperor's name, an admired British and German custom, no enquiry could be made into the how and why. This was to render democrats and liberals impotent, both morally and politically, when faced by the ultra-nationalists in the Diet or parliament in the 1930s. Maruyama pointed out that the Imperial Rescript on Education, an ultranationalist document, was proclaimed shortly before the first meeting of the parliament, and unquestionable subsequently by that parliament because the Japanese state was seen as a moral entity with an unchallengeable right to determine values. Until quite recently there was some opinion in England that the monarch and the whole royal family should personify and cement moral values.

Comparisons can at times cause worry as well as create confidence. In the 1930s opinion in the democracies was almost united that free societies paid a price in terms of efficiency compared to the modernizing autocracies like Japan and, still more so, Nazi Germany, Fascist Italy, and the Soviet Union, each claiming to be totalitarian, in complete control of their economies and, moreover, using such efficient control to rearm. But the price had to be paid, said a hundred orators and editorials. The actual conduct of the Second World War, however, showed that many of these claims were hollow. Mussolini's claims to efficiency proved empty boasts; Hitler allowed rivalry in procurement of war materials between different departments and party leaders, even rival intelligence agencies, partly through his own administrative incompetence and partly to 'divide and rule'; and Stalin with his somewhat similar paranoias (absolute power never seems to leave people feeling safe) had purged in the mid- and late 1930s somewhere between half and two-thirds of the officers of the professional army; and in Japan the breakdown in trust and contact between the army and the political leaders led to the army ignoring any political factors in determining realistic war aims. Strangely when Britain had its back to the wall and Japan attacked the United States, both countries achieved a mobilization of their economies for war greater and more efficient than in Nazi Germany. In Britain senior civil servants who before the war did not believe in planning, nor believed that it was possible, swiftly created a planned economy even including the conscription of labour, even the conscription of women. The Nazis, mainly for ideological reasons, did not conscript women until defeat stared them in the face.

How could a democracy so suddenly turn itself into an effective war economy? The answer may lie in something fundamental to free societies. Aristotle saw it way back then. How can a tyrant hope to perpetuate himself in power, he asked? And he gave a most peculiar-sounding answer. The tyrant must keep all men of ability (*arete*) 'hanging about the palace gates' and he must ban all *symposia*, those drinking and social clubs where men of any standing met in the long siesta for talk, refreshment, and whatever. Why? Well, to keep them hanging about is to keep an eye on them – marked men – and to keep them from conspiring. But why ban innocent *symposia*? Because it is in such non-political institutions that men first learn mutual trust. And without mutual trust there can be no overthrow of tyranny. I think the superior mobilization of the British war economy was because people trusted each other, decisions could be devolved, and people could work together on that basis to fulfil central plans but without constant central monitoring. (This is an art that outside times of emergency we do not now always sustain – having plenty of time to work out elaborate devices of accountability and monitoring to ensure that public servants do their jobs, which in fact interfere with them doing their jobs when trust has diminished that they can do so from their own sense of professional duty.)

I used to tell my students that Rommel as a professional soldier guessed right where the allied landings in 1944 would take place. But as Hitler fell for the bluff of the Pas de Calais rather than Normandy, so Rommel had to place his Panzers out of position, as midway between the two as he dared. Even so he had to wait three days before Hitler would agree that the Normandy landings were not a bluff. By then it was too late. I would say that if a British commander had used his initiative, disobeyed Churchill's orders, and won, he would have become, no nonsense about it, Duke of Cheltenham, Surbiton, East Ham, or such; and if he failed, Governor General of Barbados or the Falklands. But if Rommel had done similarly and failed, instant and public death; and if he had succeeded he would have had a brief season of professional esteem before being quietly removed and purged, not so much for challenging the Führer's will as for exposing Hitler's lack of omniscience. In democracies not merely can trust be greater because omniscience is not expected but also because the fruits of failure are less drastic; people will trust their arm, trust their own judgement, exercise initiative. Perhaps Lincoln thought on those lines when he said that he didn't mind if McClellan, commander of the Union armies, was conspiring to become president or dictator for the emergency, so long as he could trust him to bring victories (which he didn't, so he went). Just as the desire for revenge can run contrary to the need for political compromise, so mutual trust is a basic condition for political action, and somehow one finds more of that in democracies than in autocracies.

Chapter 7
Democratic citizenship

Then let us pray that come it may,
As come it will for a' that

  . . . . .

That man to man the warld o'er,
Shall brothers be for a' that.

(Robert Burns)

Most of the institutional devices typical of modern democracies were forged in republics or limited monarchies. Many of these pre-democratic devices were turned against the older ruling class to create a more democratic constitution, sometimes a more democratic society. It would be simple if one could say that the distinction between citizens and subjects gradually vanished – sometimes, sometimes not. In the United Kingdom the idea of legal citizenship being defined as subjects of the crown has lingered on. Immigrants seeking 'naturalization' (that is legal citizenship) have long had to take an oath of allegiance to the king or queen. Only in 2002 was a new 'citizenship oath and pledge' made law which added a pledge to respect the rights and freedoms of the United Kingdom and its inhabitants, to uphold its democratic values, observe its laws, and fulfil the duties and obligations of citizenship.

That last obligation, if somewhat ambiguous, is interesting. If the duties and obligations of citizenship simply meant the traditional obeying of the laws in return for the protection of the laws (or as some would say, being a good citizen), then that has been said already and the words are redundant. So it seems to imply a more active role for a citizen; that there is a duty to respect the rights and freedoms found in the United Kingdom. Political philosophers would argue that there is a close, even a reciprocal relationship between rights and duties: that you and I cannot assert what we conceive to be our rights without implying a duty to consider what effects this may have on others and thus to respect and encourage the rights of others; similarly if you and I pursue what we may conceive to be our path of civic duty, it implies that we think others

12. Nelson Mandela casts his vote in the first non-racial, full democratic election in South Africa, 1994.

have a similar duty and should be given the knowledge, skills and opportunities to exercise such duties. So it sounds as if the Home Office, whether consciously as government policy or unconsciously following perhaps a changing spirit in our times (the Germans have one word for this, *zeitgeist*), are saying that to be a new British immigrant citizen you must be, or should recognize that you ought to be, an active citizen. A republican paradigm has been grafted onto a monarchical one. In the USA there has long been a citizenship exam for immigrants and a ceremony in front of the flag pledging allegiance to the constitution. Having a written constitution in a democracy, even if it was, strictly speaking, a pre-democratic constitution, makes any dismissive distinction between the rights of legal citizenship and the expected duties of citizenship harder to draw – at least on paper.

Institutions

To be effective, active citizenship demands not just will and skill but some knowledge of institutions, not an abstract or an academic comprehensive knowledge, but a practical knowledge of what levers of power are relevant to particular intentions. It would be far beyond the scope of this book to try to compare the relevant effectiveness of different forms of institution in different democracies. Political scientists do a lot of this, but I have always been sceptical about whether there is ever a like to compare with a like once one appreciates how much the same thing works differently in the context of different national cultures and histories. The United Kingdom in the post-war period of withdrawal from empire gave or left behind Westminster models of parliamentary government in nearly all her former colonies. None work as expected, some broke down entirely, and even where they didn't (as most notably in India) a prior knowledge of Westminster ways could be a prejudicial obstacle rather than a help in understanding the new context, dynamics, problems, and possibilities.

However, there are some general institutional characteristics of modern democracies. Some are obvious, some less so; but let me set them down nevertheless. I base this, with homage but paraphrasing with amendment and addition, on the categories in Professor Robert Dahl's fine article in *The International Encyclopedia of the Social and Behavioral Sciences*, even if I differ with him on his assertion that most of these are specifically modern.

- *Elected representatives.* Control of government by members of a parliament or assembly etc. elected by citizens. Actually Dahl says 'elected officials' which is either rare or quite specific to many parts of the USA. (When judges and state prosecutors are elected, then the populist mode of democracy rather than the liberal democratic has kicked in.)
- *Free, fair, and frequent elections.* He adds 'in which coercion is relatively rare'. Teams of election observers now go out to many countries trying to establish or re-establish democratic elections after emerging from military dictatorship; they look for coercion but also for fraud (which may not be unknown at home).
- *Freedom of expression.* 'Citizens have a right to express themselves without danger of severe punishment on political matters broadly defined . . .'. Indeed, but is 'political' needed here? Some suppression of free speech in autocracies takes place by branding words as 'political', certainly; but it can also be said ingenuously that the banning of sex education in public high schools is *not* political – simply a matter of the private morality of school boards, parents, and even legislators not subject to political compromises
- *Access to alternative, independent sources of information.* Dahl is right to put this immediately after 'freedom of expression', which becomes useless if sources of evidence are not available to challenge governments' publications and their ability to massage, suppress, or even invent statistics, especially if the governments have undue influence, even control, over the press and broadcasting media.
- *Autonomous associations.* Citizens must have 'the right to form relatively independent associations or organisations, including

independent political parties and interest groups'. Indeed, following Tocqueville, this is fundamental to freedom and democracy; but it seems that political parties in modern democracies are the basic institutions that bind government to the electorate. So 'a multi-party' system may deserve a separate title. And issues of how far new demands for multicultural policies can go are complex and not easy (as are self-portraits about how multicultural are states like Britain and the USA already).

· *Inclusive citizenship.* 'No adult permanently residing in the country and subject to its laws can be denied the rights that are available to citizens and are necessary to the five political institutions listed above.' But note that the right to vote is often not granted to permanent residents. National feelings can run high. And laws on the status of foreign spouses can often be highly specific and peculiar.

However, perhaps Robert Dahl takes for granted what is not to be taken for granted, especially in new or emerging democracies: the need for some real *independence of the judiciary* from government and some real constitutional support for *an impartial and reasonably neutral civil service*. Perhaps he would answer that because the United States is plainly a democracy *without* these two institutional features, that they are not prerequisites at all. I would grant the relative singularity of American institutions but then see this lack as an element of populist democracy rejected by others in the name of good government. But the western US states nearly all legislated in the 1900s for some quite interesting devices attempting to secure a populist style of politics: provisions for *initiative* of legislation by popular petition, for *referenda*, and for *recall* of elected members. Not all have survived and their blessings have been very mixed.

So we circle round and round this point. As soon as we think we have at least an ostensive or empirical definition of democracy – that is pointing to common features of regimes normally called democracies – we find the majoritarian or populist problem arising.

Plato's ghost haunts us. Yes, we know the answer. History, reason, and morality must throw into the democratic pot liberty, human rights, and the brotherhood of man. This good blend we then can cheerfully label as modern democracy, even if the label is better than much of the wine. So to avoid fatuous optimism that this blending always equates with good government, should we not, while we are about any listing such as above, add these two other negative requirements for good government: that neither an American-style party 'spoils system' for public officials nor a politically motivated judiciary are conducive to political justice, and sometimes not even to political stability? And democracies can be as foolish, reckless, and aggressive in their foreign policies as can autocracies. There are no final answers in the name of democracy. Lists, like definitions, settle nothing. There is only a continual process of compromise between different values and interests, politics itself.

What people see as democratic principles may sometimes have to be compromised. The Revd Dr Ian Paisley, MP, MEP frequently and understandably complains Northern Ireland is governed in an undemocratic manner: 'the democratic' majority is denied power by an imposed, highly artificial, and intricate power-sharing arrangement based on a contrived electoral system; and the imposition connived at, to make matters worse, by a foreign government; so both national sovereignty and democratic principles are broken. Indeed, but what was being sought after (as Thomas Hobbes would have sardonically recognized) was peace, not pure democracy, something perhaps not agreeable to a majority but at least acceptable. It was, indeed, a political process, not a fully democratic one. In South Africa around the time of transition from a racist state to a negotiated democratic constitution, the African National Congress raised the cry of 'one person, one vote' (actually they said 'one man, one vote', but quickly erased that small error). There was no possible denying their right and power to the vote and to make South African blacks the overwhelming majority in the new order. But that was not the whole point. Their leaders knew that there had not merely to be a peaceful resolution but one that would not cause a flight of investment and capital from South Africa. Therefore formidable legal restraints and a Bill of Rights became part of the political compromises of the new constitution specifically to reassure white South Africans. In some ways 'the Peace Commission' (no punishments for past violations of human rights in return for true confessions) could be seen as a denial of principles of justice and of majority rights; but again it was a compromise for the sake of peace and economic and political stability. Democracy returned to Spain and Chile with somewhat similar compromises. 'Sovereignty of the people' was recognized to have limits. The safety and future of the republic, of republican or democratic government, in both cases was put before the great risks involved in pursuing vengeance, even justice, against the perpetrators of atrocities, violators of human rights.

Liberalism and republicanism

Most people today want to keep their engagements with the state and public affairs to the minimum. We enjoy the benefits of known and acceptable laws (unless very poor or otherwise discriminated against). The liberal state as it developed in the last two centuries in Europe and North America created a framework within which people could lead their private and commercial lives with a minimum of interference. Their interventions were limited in the main to voting in public elections. Relatively few people outside the labour movements were active in political parties; most were content to leave public affairs to a relatively small group of people under the scrutiny of the press and, to some extent at least, under the control of the courts. That political class consisted sometimes of democratic socialists representative of a majority working-class movement or sometimes of Conservatives or Christian Democrats accepting or developing enough of a welfare state to defuse discontent with the system. Between them there were serious policy differences centring on attempts to redistribute income, somewhat – but never to kill the goose that was laying golden eggs, the capitalist market system. Business interests resented higher taxation for political or moral ends and often talked hysterically about the very system of private enterprise being near collapse, which was never so. But there came a time when the success of post-war capitalism had created a middle class larger than the old working class, in large part a new middle class able to spend money on consumer goods, cutting adrift from the old world of essentials, bare necessities, and hard saving against emergencies. In Britain the co-operative stores were replaced by the supermarkets. This was the consumer society. Thatcherism and Reaganism did not create it. They were products of it. They could now win elections without bothering too much about the welfare of a working class who were no longer, for the first time in history, the majority class, indeed were rapidly becoming an under-class – depoliticized, unorganized, and no longer protected by the competitive party systems of democracy.

Party leaders could conduct election campaigns by brushing aside difficult issues with nebulous sincerities but with no real serious debate. The parties concentrated their efforts on the middle ground: lower taxation replaced public expenditure as election cries. The new middle class was far more individualistic than the older middle class, more self-and-family centred with less feeling for public service, less belief that rights entail duties and responsibilities. Party leaders and managers became openly and unashamedly more interested in immediate election tactics, projection of personality, and in media presentation than in thinking through and advocating ideas and policies relating to long-term social needs. Many of those urban intellectuals who were once so influential in social democratic politics now take up big small causes such as 'Save the Whale', 'Ban GM Foods', animal rights, etc., but not poverty or economic injustice. They will attack racism as, indeed, an affront to human dignity and any kind of democracy, but not face up to the root causes of discrimination – stark poverty, economic disadvantage, and even relative deprivation. Political leaders in Britain who had been wont on platforms and in memoirs to ascribe British democracy and freedoms to the great traditions of service in local government and in voluntary bodies, suddenly began to downgrade and even rubbish local government as a wild card in national politics and election strategies, and make speeches aimed at reviving volunteering – good for the soul, certainly, but also for savings on government services and a further undercutting of local government which was not so long ago believed to be at the very roots of democracy. And in the United States the terrible events of 11 September 2001 became an excuse to excite popular passions to indifference to the once-great tradition of constitutional and civil rights.

Now I have lapsed into putting in somewhat populist terms what political thinkers would express more soberly and theoretically as the difference between liberal democracy and the older civic republic ideas of the duty of citizens to participate in public affairs; and that so doing in concert with others is a moral education. In Britain and the United States we are, in fact, in at least the second decade of a remarkable spread and revival of serious political thought. The only difficulty is that it is confined to the universities, academics talking to each other and their brighter students (it is not a soft option like most business studies). Little of it penetrates to politicians or the press. Quentin Skinner, a leading historian of political ideas, has written that 'it is ironic that the development of the Western democracies should have been accompanied by the atrophying of the ideal that government of the people should be conducted by the people'.

> Among moral and political writers of the Renaissance, it was widely agreed that the only way to maximise the liberty of individual citizens must be to ensure that everyone plays an active role in political affairs. Only by such full participation, it was argued, can we hope to prevent the business of government falling into the hands of a ruling class. Since the seventeenth century, however, the leading Western democracies have repudiated this view in favour of a strongly contrasting one. It has been an axiom of liberal theories

about the relationship between government and the governed that the only way to maximise freedom must be to minimize the extent to which public demands can legitimately be made on our private lives.

I would only differ with the rigidity of the time-scales he implies. This civic republicanism existed strongly in the early American republic but was swept away as a popular force in the 'triumphant' democratic capitalism of the post-civil-war era; and something of this positive approach to liberty or freedom was common in the Chartist and Labour movements: freedom was not just being free from interference, it was *acting freely* for the public good or the general interest. But this does not detract from the broad point he makes. The very scale of the political and legal institutions of modern democracies seems to demand the good citizen more than the active citizen: the relatively smooth working and security of democratic institutions can actually smother an active democratic spirit by appearing to diminish its need. Nearly all significant measures of public participation in political processes now show marked decline, not merely in election turn-outs.

Citizenship

The question should finally be asked, essentially Rousseau's question, can we educate for a democracy? And what examples from government can help or hinder? It happens that I was made chairman of an advisory group to a Secretary of State for Education with the remit: 'To promote advice on effective education for citizenship in schools – to include the nature and practices of participation in democracy; the duties, responsibilities and rights of individuals as citizens; and the value to individuals and society of community activity'. 'An effective education for citizenship' and 'practices of participation', that was a remit I could live with at the small price of temporary silence about the contrast (contradiction?) between these incitements and the government's general style or policy of centralization and tight control, especially within its own party. Fortunately governments are not wholly consistent. They want, of course, good behaviour and *good* citizens, but also (Quentin Skinner and I are at times too gloomy) the old language and aspirations of *active* citizenship or civic republicanism keeps breaking out in some key contexts – like in the new oath to gain legal citizenship and in the remit to my committee. The eventual report was unanimous and was adopted as a new and compulsory curriculum in English secondary schools. It stated:

> We aim at no less than a change in the political culture of this country both nationally and locally: for people to think of themselves as active citizens, willing, able and equipped to have an influence in public life and with the critical capacities to weigh evidence before speaking and acting; to build on and to extend radically to young people the best in existing traditions of community involvement and public service, and to make them individually confident in finding new forms of involvement and action among themselves.

I often wonder how many of my group realized that they were signing up to the radical agenda of civic republicanism rather than the less demanding 'good citizen' and 'rule of law' imperatives of liberal democracy. The 'citizenship order' for schools provides instrumentalities for this more radical agenda: discussion of controversial issues; participation in school and community affairs; learning skills of advocacy; the idea of 'political literacy' as a blending of skills, knowledge, and attitudes; learning awareness of cultural diversities – the different nations, religions, and ethnic groups within the United Kingdom; all this and more where there was no national curriculum for citizenship before. I often wonder if the government as a whole realized the gradual but real effects this could have on society (if it has much effect at all, which is now in the hands of teachers not governments) and on the conduct of government itself. People might become more demanding and more knowledgeable about how to achieve their demands, also irritatingly more unpredictable. From a government's point of view the trouble with free citizens is that a government is never quite sure how they will exercise that freedom.

Some leading politicians in both countries try to bridge the contradiction between the convenience of liberal democratic theory for the conduct of government and the more disruptive, unpredictable civic republican theory. They try to reduce, whether sincerely or cynically, citizenship to 'volunteering', or in the USA 'service learning'. But the difficulty is this: too much volunteering can simply be young people being told what to do by well-meaning older folk. Volunteers can be canon fodder and can become disillusioned if they are not treated as citizens and are given responsibilities for carrying out a task but not for suggesting how to modify it if it seems mistaken or trivial either in aims or methods.

Most countries in Western Europe already had citizenship education in their schools, and now countries from the former Soviet bloc add it to their curricula, almost desperate to counter the cynicism about government created by decades of indoctrination rather than education. The UK now sees the need and has acted, and the USA is setting about restoring, repairing, and hopefully reforming (not conforming – too early to tell) civic education in its public high schools. The main motive may be to restore or create *good* citizenship but generally it is realized that that can only be a welcome by-product of learning *active* citizenship, aiming to empower young people. The old routines of learning about 'the constitution' in a non-discussive, un-problematic, and therefore dead boring manner (often called Civics) are now generally recognized as at least useless, at worst counter-productive to encouraging a democratic spirit. Even in the heart of consumer societies, even with the dispiriting examples set by those in public life, there is this small mediating tendency, potentially important; or at least a sign that the ideas of civic republicanism in the context of democratic institutions are, if not in the ascendancy, not yet vanquished by any means, as the historian of ideas implies. Some good people are doing it without having read about it.

In conclusion

All discussions of democracy are inconclusive and never-ending. Fortunately there are no final solutions, hellish or benign, the Holocaust or a New Jerusalem on earth. There is in the emergence of global capitalism but 'no end of history', as Fukiyama foolishly argued. Capitalism is as strong or as brittle as the moral sense and responsibility of capitalists (the somewhat forgotten part of the teaching of Adam Smith in *The Wealth of Nations*). 'Sovereign states' are not as sovereign (if some of them ever were) or as powerful as in the past, but the political modifications they can achieve in their economies are not insignificant to their inhabitants. In some respects the world situation is depressing.

13. The Berlin Wall, 8 November 1989.

It is not particularly safe for democracy, as was Woodrow Wilson's ideal. Neither the United Nations nor the United States has the inclination or the power to try to impose democracy, or even human rights, universally. And there is no democracy between states, and others can vote as they choose in international forums, but the present government of the United States puts domestic lobbies before concerted action on global warming, peace keeping, joining on equal terms an international court for war crimes; and 'the war against terrorism' proves ludicrously arbitrary.

The reasons to hope for the spread of democratic *institutions* are mainly to be found in important negative arguments: the tendency for economic inefficiency and wasteful corruption in one-party states or military regimes whose conduct of government and plans are not subject to public criticism. Such regimes can collapse literally into bankruptcy and by massive inflations of worthless currencies that can finally provoke their people into rebellion and the supporters of their state apparatus into inactive despair. The people involved in the risings in Eastern Europe in November 1989 acted heroically. There was a democratic *spirit*, indeed. The workers, the church congregations, and the students in Leipzig, Dresden, Berlin, Prague, and Bratislava, etc. did not know that the police and the army would not fire on them (sometimes disobeying orders to fire). The 'power of the people' and human courage was demonstrated, even if they only hastened not caused the collapse of those regimes. The Communist Party in the Soviet Union tried to reform in time by *glasnost* and *perestroika* and to retain power in a more benign guise, but the whole economic system simply broke down. Revolutions as often take place because the old regime simply collapses out of economic inefficiency and bureaucratic rigidity rather than for the reasons given out by their successors taking too much credit, however heroic their actions at the time of crisis (but so often in the past hopeless). To mock old Marxists, there are 'objective reasons' why democratic economies are usually stronger.

But China makes one pause. Those who argue, as the late F. A. Hayek did so powerfully, that capitalism created democracy and even that globalization is thus a force for the inevitability of democracy, have some special pleading to do over the case of the most rapidly expanding capitalist economy in the world in which the government nonetheless remains in the hands of a party that represses any expression of political opposition; albeit a government that has, as it were, retreated both from detailed controls of society and egalitarianism doctrine, as distinct from a meritocratic ethos. Can the success of the economy divert the minds of the Chinese people away from political and democratic questions entirely – a stark modern example of the Roman imperial 'bread and circuses' – or will corruption, dissension, and damaging mistakes emerge at the top? Perhaps the real story of democracy in the West (not Hayek's – he somehow forgot about the pre-capitalist Greeks and the Romans) is when elites begin to quarrel among themselves for absolute mastery (power does that to people), and one faction or another appeals to the power of the people, whoever the people are who have potential powers, whether on the streets or in boardrooms of banks and trading companies.

My own views are fairly clear, I hope; but all things are relative and even a purely liberal democratic regime aggressively supporting a largely depoliticized consumer capitalism would be preferable to an old-style Soviet or even a new China model. We can do better than that, however. Circumstances change and there are always choices for change that can be made, always some influence that can be applied if we know the pressure points; changes do not always come as quickly as we might wish, sometimes too quickly. But in a modern democracy changes can be made and are best made not in a populist manner but in a reasoned political manner. Politicians who want to be followed know that they have to listen. That's democracy for you.

Can existing 'democracies' become radically more democratic societies? Improved institutional arrangements are always needed but are never enough by themselves to induce a democratic spirit. The answer in theory is fairly obvious: the diffusion of power. Take the case of Britain and Europe. There is plainly a strong case for some powers to be devolved down, but others quite rightly were devolved up. Some big things we could not do on our own, but in many other things there is no need for uniformity whether coming from Brussels or Whitehall and Westminster (or should one add, Washington?). David Marquand has put the theory of this most eloquently. Wilson of Pennsylvania was in 1787 right: 'He was for raising the federal pyramid to a considerable altitude, and for that reason wished to give it as broad a base as possible'. Within Britain itself there are, after all, good reasons why the economy has become over a long period more and more centralized. There are great benefits in the enterprise economy of a liberal democratic state and problems of scale make the ancient ideas of civic democracy, of civic republicanism, and a 'face-to-face' society hard to apply. Communication, availability of information, transparency and open government, the press and the broadcasting media, these are in reality controls on central government more powerful than direct participation. But the reasons why the powers of local government have been diminished have been almost wholly bad.

Civic republicanism, that is the democratic spirit of direct participation, can and should be firmly rooted in regions, localities, neighbourhoods; and all powers that can be devolved should be devolved. One cannot have both freedom and uniformity. For example, our national press in Britain clamours that it is a 'postcode' lottery whether or not one can get a particular treatment on the National Health Service, or how quickly. But the papers also clamour (on another day) against rigid, bureaucratic centralism. Governments who believe that the press is public opinion, or can influence it more than they can, then produce national standards or frameworks that give no space for serious thought and action about local needs, priorities, and initiatives. Fear of the arbitrariness of the press also inhibits serious debate about division of powers between centre and localities, indeed also between what is appropriate to public and what to private provision. Tocqueville was right. A high degree of autonomy for localities and groups within the state is essential for freedom within a democracy. So thought the civic republicans, remembering the Greeks and the Romans: within sub-groups and localities wherever possible and as far as possible participative democracy should be practised. Such is good for the polity and good for the life of each individual. We are at our best as others see us, which depends, of course, on how we see them – morally, politically, democratically.

I am a humanist. But I am in sympathy with much that was in the theologian Reinhold Niebuhr's book *Christian Realism and Political Problems*: 'Man's inclination to justice makes democracy possible; but man's capacity for injustice makes it necessary.' The optimism we need to prevent ourselves from destroying our own democratic freedoms and, indeed, our own human habitat must be based on a reasoned pessimism.

Further reading

Nearly everything written on the history of political ideas either touches on democracy or is relevant to it, and similarly the vast number of general books on types of political institutions – whether called, at various times, 'Modern Democracies' or not. In the United States particularly the whole study of politics can revolve around the meanings and the institutions of democracy (to a fault, for if we are to combat other systems we need to understand how they actually work; and to avoid thinking that how we practise democracy is the only game in town). So I have decided to be ruthlessly, but I hope then helpfully, selective: I now list the books I myself have used and found helpful over many years and in writing this long essay or short book. There are so many truths that one must be economical.

For classic works I have not recommended particular editions. Scholarly editions are to be found in the magnificently comprehensive, ongoing series of the Cambridge Texts in the History of Political Thought (Cambridge University Press); but there are a wide variety of more popular paperback editions also.

Advisory Group on Citizenship, *Education for Citizenship and the Teaching of Democracy in Schools* (Qualifications and Curriculum Authority, 1998).

Horatio Alger, *Struggling Upward, or Luke Larkin's Luck*, ed. Carl Bode (Penguin Books, 1985).

Geoff Andrews (ed.), *Citizenship* (Lawrence & Wishart, 1991).

Hannah Arendt, *The Origins of Totalitarianism*, 2nd edn (Allen & Unwin, 1958).

—— *The Human Condition* (Cambridge University Press, 1958).

Aristotle, *The Politics*.

—— *Main Currents in Sociological Thought*, vol. 1 (Weidenfeld & Nicolson, 1965).

Raymond Aron, *Democracy and Totalitarianism* (Weidenfeld & Nicolson, 1968).

Benjamin Barber, *Strong Democracy* (University of California Press, 1984).

Max Beloff (ed.), *The Debate on the American Revolution, 1761–1783* (Nicholas Kaye, 1949).

Isaiah Berlin, *Four Essays on Liberty* (Oxford University Press, 1969).

J. H. Burns, *Political Thought: 1450–1700* (Cambridge University Press, 1991).

Andrew Carnegie, *Triumphant Democracy* (1886).

Alfred Cobban, *The Debate on the French Revolution, 1789–1800* (Nicholas Kaye, 1950).

Benjamin Constant, *Écrits politiques*, ed. Marcel Gauchet (Éditions Gallimard, 1997).

F. R. Cowell, *Cicero and the Roman Republic* (Pelican Books, 1956).

Bernard Crick (ed.), *Citizens: Towards a Citizenship Culture* (Blackwell and Political Quarterly, 2001).

—— *Essays on Citizenship* (Continuum, 2000).

—— *In Defence of Politics*, 5th edn (Continuum, 2000).

—— *Basic Forms of Government* (Macmillan, 1973).

Colin Crouch, *Coping with Post-Democracy* (Fabian Society, 2001).

—— and David Marquand (eds), *Reinventing Collective Action* (Blackwell and *Political Quarterly*, 1992).

Robert A. Dahl, *Democracy and Its Critics* (Yale University Press, 1991).

—— *On Democracy* (Yale University Press, 1999).

Cynthia Farrar, *The Origins of Democratic Thinking: The Invention of Politics in Classical Athens* (Cambridge University Press, 1988).

S. E. Finer, *The Man on Horseback* (Pall Mall Press, 1962).

—— *The History of Government*, 3 vols (Oxford University Press, 1997).

M. I. Finley, *The Ancient Greeks* (Chatto & Windus, 1963).

W. G. Forrest, *The Emergence of Greek Democracy* (Weidenfeld & Nicolson, 1966).

Carl J. Friedrich, *Constitutional Government and Democracy*, rev. edn (Ginn & Co., New York, 1950).

Andrew Gamble, *Politics and Fate* (Polity, 2000).

Ernest Gellner, *Conditions of Liberty: Civil Society and Its Rivals* (Hamish Hamilton, 1994).

Alexander Hamilton, John Jay, and James Madison, *The Federalist*

James Harrington, *Oceana – see* J. G. A. Pocock.

Louis Hartz, *The Liberal Tradition in America* (Harcourt Brace, 1955).

David Held, *Models of Democracy*, 2nd edn (Polity, 1996).

Christopher Hill, *Puritanism and Revolution* (Secker & Warburg, 1958).

Paul Hirst and Sunil Khilnani, *Reinventing Democracy* (Blackwell and *Political Quarterly*, 1996).

Thomas Hobbes, *Leviathan* (1651).

Richard Hofstadter, *The Paranoid Style in American Politics* (Cape, 1966).

Thomas Jefferson, *Political Writings*, ed. Joyce Oldham Appleby and Terence Ball (Cambridge University Press, 1996).

John Keane, *Democracy and Civil Society* (Verso, 1988).

Preston King, *Toleration* (Allen & Unwin, 1976).

Mario Attilio Levi, *Political Power in the Ancient World* (Weidenfeld & Nicolson, 1965).

A. D. Lindsay, *The Modern Democratic State* (Oxford University Press, 1943).

John Locke, *Two Treatises on Government* (1689).

Niccolò Machiavelli, *The Discourses* (1531).

C. H. McIlwain, *Constitutionalism Ancient and Modern* (Cornell University Press, 1947).

C. B. Macpherson, *The Real World of Democracy* (Oxford University Press, 1966).

David Marquand, *The New Reckoning: Society, State and Citizens* (Polity, 1997).

Masao Maruyama, *Thought and Behaviour in Modern Japanese Politics*, ed. Ivan Morris (Oxford University Press, 1963).

Lidia Storoni Mazzolani, *The Idea of the City in Roman Thought* (Hollis & Carter, 1967).

Christian Meier, *The Greek Discovery of Politics* (Harvard University Press, 1990).

Michael Mendle (ed.), *The Putney Debates of 1647: the Army, the Levellers and the British State* (Cambridge University Press, 2001).

J. S. Mill, *Autobiography* (1873).

—— *On Liberty* (1859).

—— *Considerations on Representative Government* (1861).

Barrington Moore Jnr., *Social Origins of Dictatorship and Democracy* (Allen Lane, 1967).

Reinhold Niebuhr, *Christian Realism and Political Problems* (Faber & Faber, 1954).

Adrian Oldfield, *Citizenship and Community: Civic Republicanism and the Modern World* (Routledge, 1990).

Dawn Oliver and Derek Heater, *The Foundations of Citizenship* (Harvester Wheatsheaf, 1994).

Plato, *The Republic*.

J. G. A. Pocock (ed.), *The Political Works of James Harrington* (Cambridge University Press, 1977).

—— *The Machiavellian Moment: Florentine Political Thought and the Atlantic Republican Tradition* (Princeton University Press, 1975).

John Rawls, *A Theory of Justice* (Clarendon Press, 1972).

Joseph Schumpeter, *Capitalism, Socialism and Democracy* (Allen & Unwin, 1943).

Richard Sennett, *The Fall of Public Man* (Knopf, 1977).

Quentin Skinner, *Liberty Before Liberalism* (Cambridge University Press, 1998).

Adam Smith, *The Wealth of Nations* (1776).

Herbert Spencer, *Man versus the State* (1884).

John Tebbel, *From Rags to Riches: Horatio Alger, Jr. and the American Dream* (New York, Macmillan, 1965).

Thucydides, *The Peloponnesian War*.

Alexis de Tocqueville, *L'Ancien Régime et la Révolution en France* (1856), translated under various titles.

—— *Democracy in America*, 2 vols. (1835–40).

H. G. Wells, *The Future in America* (Harper, 1906).

Index

Expand your collection of
VERY SHORT INTRODUCTIONS

Visit the

VERY SHORT
INTRODUCTIONS

Web site

www.oup.co.uk/vsi

➤ **Information** about all published titles

➤ News of **forthcoming books**

➤ **Extracts** from the books, including titles
not yet published

➤ **Reviews** and views

➤ **Links** to other **web sites** and main
OUP web page

➤ Information about **VSIs in translation**

➤ **Contact** the editors

➤ **Order** other **VSIs** on-line

POLITICS
A Very Short Introduction
Kenneth Minogue

In this provocative but balanced essay, Kenneth Minogue discusses the development of politics from the ancient world to the twentieth century. He prompts us to consider why political systems evolve, how politics offers both power and order in our society, whether democracy is always a good thing, and what future politics may have in the twenty-first century.

'This is a fascinating book which sketches, in a very short space, one view of the nature of politics … the reader is challenged, provoked and stimulated by Minogue's trenchant views.'

Ian Davies, *Talking Politics*

'a dazzling but unpretentious display of great scholarship and humane reflection'

Neil O'Sullivan, University of Hull

www.oup.co.uk/vsi/politics

T... ...y Short Introduction to Classics links a haunting temple on a lonely mountainside to the glory of ancient Greece and the grandeur of Rome, and to Classics within modern culture – from Jefferson and Byron to Asterix and Ben-Hur.

'The authors show us that Classics is a "modern" and sexy subject. They succeed brilliantly in this regard … nobody could fail to be informed and entertained – and the accent of the book is provocative and stimulating.'

John Godwin, *Times Literary Supplement*

'Statues and slavery, temples and tragedies, museum, marbles, and mythology – this provocative guide to the Classics demysties its varied subject-matter while seducing the reader with the obvious enthusiasm and pleasure which mark its writing.'

Edith Hall

www.ou... .co.uk